Python: The Ultimate Beginners Guide

Start Coding Today

Preface

I'm aware that learning a new programming language can be a gargantuan task. This is most especially true for individuals who have yet to know the basic elements of computer programming. This dilemma is universal, and is perfectly understood by the author.

Hence, the presentation of the contents in this book is done in an easy-to-understand language. This would help you comprehend better. In addition, the simple instructions will ensure that the procedures are understood first, before they are executed, or run.

Let's make sure, you make the most out of this new information. All you need to do is to be open-minded, and be willing to learn.

I hope you enjoy it!

© Copyright 2016 by Steve Tale All rights reserved.

This document is geared towards providing exact and reliable information in regards to the topic and issue covered. The publication is sold with the idea that the publisher is not required to render accounting, officially permitted, or otherwise, qualified services. If advice is necessary, legal or professional, a practiced individual in the profession should be ordered.

- From a Declaration of Principles which was accepted and approved equally by a Committee of the American Bar Association and a Committee of Publishers and Associations.

In no way is it legal to reproduce, duplicate, or transmit any part of this document in either electronic means or in printed format. Recording of this publication is strictly prohibited and any storage of this document is not allowed unless with written permission from the publisher. All rights reserved.

The information provided herein is stated to be truthful and consistent, in that any liability, in terms of inattention or otherwise, by any usage or abuse of any policies, processes, or directions contained within is the solitary and utter responsibility of the recipient reader. Under no circumstances will any legal responsibility or blame be held against the publisher for any reparation, damages, or monetary loss due to the information herein, either directly or indirectly.

Respective authors own all copyrights not held by the publisher.

The information herein is offered for informational purposes solely, and is universal as so. The presentation of the information is without contract or any type of guarantee assurance.

The trademarks that are used are without any consent, and the publication of the trademark is without permission or backing by the trademark owner. All trademarks and brands within this book are for clarifying purposes only and are the owned by the owners themselves, not affiliated with this document.

Contents

Preface 2

Chapter 1: Introduction to Python 7

Chapter 2: How to Install Python.. 9

Chapter 3: Basic Python Terms You Must Learn.................. 17

Chapter 4: Functions of the Python Standard Library 24

Chapter 5: Basic Elements of Python 31

Chapter 6: Types of Python Statements 35

Chapter 7: How to Start Using Python 45

Chapter 8: Basic Python Syntax Rules 55

Chapter 9: Application of Python in Math and Numbers 64

Chapter 10: Using Variables and Assigning Values 71

Chapter 11: Learning the Built-in Modules and Functions 76

Chapter 12: Creating, Saving and Running Python Files 83

Chapter 13: Utilizing User-Defined Functions 93

Chapter 14: How to Use and Define a Class 98

Chapter 15: Creating & Accessing Your Python Dictionary 110

Chapter 16: Creating and Combining Strings 116

Chapter 17: Accessing and Updating Strings 131

Chapter 18: Built-in Functions to Format Strings 137

Chapter 19: Symbols and Operators in Formatting Strings 145

Chapter 20: Important Python Semantics 148

Chapter 21: Operators and Their Functions 150

Chapter 22: Using 'IF ELSE' Statements.............................155

Chapter 23: Using ELIF Statements 160

Chapter 24: Functions of Python Loops..............................164

Chapter 25: Creating and Using Tuples..............................170

Chapter 26: How to Convert Python Data..........................185

Chapter 27: How to Build Your Python Lists.......................192

Chapter 28: Slicing from a List...198

Chapter 29: Short Quiz on Python Programming 211

Chapter 30: Answers to Short Quiz....................................213

Chapter 31: Pointers in Using Python Programming 230

Conclusion 233

Bonus: Preview Of 'SQL The Ultimate Beginners Guide Learn SQL Today..234

Chapter 1: Introduction to Python

In this generation of computer programming and highly technical applications, it's smart to move with the times. If you don't, you will be left behind in many undertakings that you want to pursue.

If you want to be the cream of the crop, you must learn how to create and read computer or programming language. Your knowledge will not only set you apart from your contemporaries, but will also boost your productivity and self-advancement in relevance with the expanding world of computer lingo.

What is Python?

Python is a powerful programming language. You can use it for free in developing software that can run on Nokia mobile phones, Windows, Mac OS X, Linux, Unix, JAVA, Amiga, and many more operating systems.

Python is object-oriented and provides simple and easy to read and use language that you can utilize in creating your programs.

Even if you're not a programmer, it would be beneficial for you to know about Python because of the numerous uses you can take advantage of.

So, where is Python used?

Here is a summary of the uses of Python:

1. To process images
2. To write Internet scripts
3. To embed scripts

4. To manipulate database programs
5. To provide system utilities
6. To create artificial intelligence
7. To create graphical user interface applications using IDEs on Windows and other platforms

Advantages of learning Python

For you to understand more what you stand to gain from learning Python, here are its major pros.

You can:

1. Learn Python easily because the syntax or language in programming is simple.
2. Prepare codes readily that can be used in various operating systems such as Linux, Windows, Unix and Mac OS X.
3. Promptly access the Python standard library that helps users in creating, editing, accessing, running and maintaining files.
4. Integrate programs and systems promptly because the programming language is easy to follow.
5. Handle the errors more reliably because the syntax is capable of identifying and raising exceptions.
6. Learn more quickly because the programming language is object oriented.
7. Access IDLE, which makes it possible for users to create codes and check if the codes work, through Python's interactive system.
8. Download Python for free, and enjoy all the benefits of a free application.
9. Embed your Python data in other systems.
10. Stop worrying about freeing the memory for your codes, because Python does it automatically.

If you're in, then, let's start the ball rolling!

Chapter 2: How to Install Python

In this time and age, being techy is a demand of the times, and the lack of knowledge, classifies one as an outback. This can result to being left out from the career world, especially in the field of programming.

Numerous big shot companies have employed their own programmers for purposes of branding, and to cut back on IT expenses.

In the world of programming, using Python language is found to be easier and programmer-friendly, thus, the universal use.

Discussed below are information on how to download python for MS Windows. In this particular demo, we have chosen windows because it's the most common worldwide – even in not so progressive countries. We want to cater to the programming needs of everyone all over the globe.

Python 2.7.12 version was selected because this version bridges the gap between the old version 2 and the new version 3.

Some of the updated functions/applications of version 3 are still not compatible with some devices, so 2.7.12 is a smart choice.

Steps in downloading Python 2.7.12, and installing it on Windows

1. Type python on your browser and press the Search button to display the search results.

   Scroll down to find the item you are interested in. In this instance, you are looking for python. click "python releases for windows", and a new page opens. See image below:

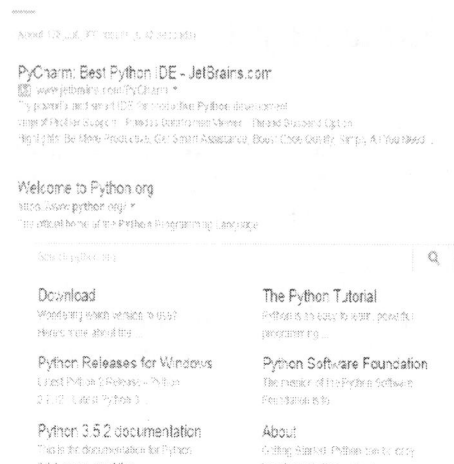

2. Select the Python version, python 2.7.12, and click, or you can select the version that is compatible to your device or OS.

3. The new page contains the various python types. Scroll down and select an option: in this instance, select Windows x86 MSI installer and click.

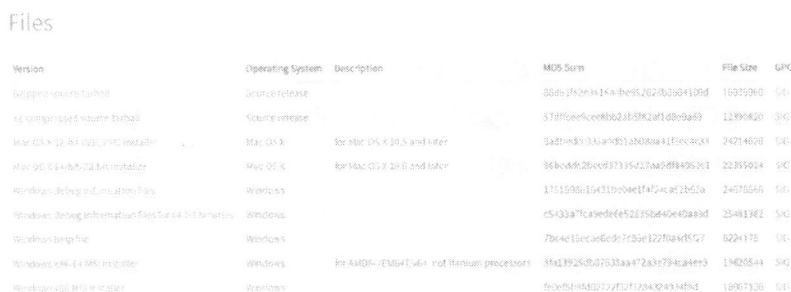

4. Press the Python box at the bottom of your screen.

Click the "Run" button, and wait for the new window to appear.

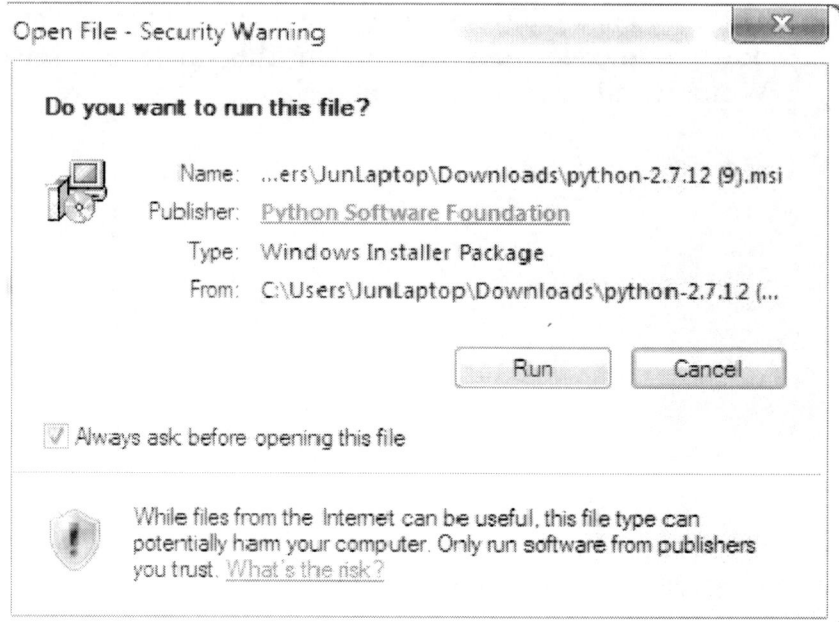

5. Select the user options that you require and press "NEXT".

Your screen will display the hard drive where your python will be located.

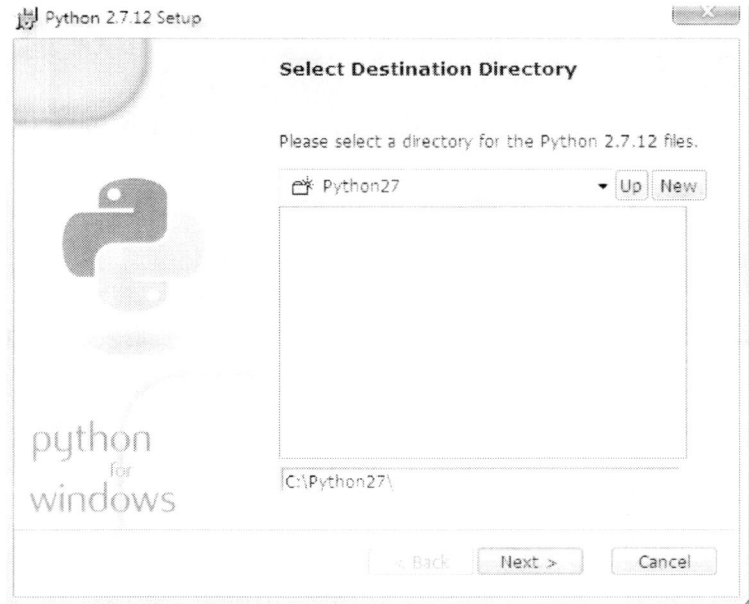

6. Press the "NEXT" button.

7. Press yes, and wait for a few minutes. Sometimes it can take longer for the application to download, depending on the speed of your internet.

8. After that, click the FINISHED button to signify that the installation has been completed

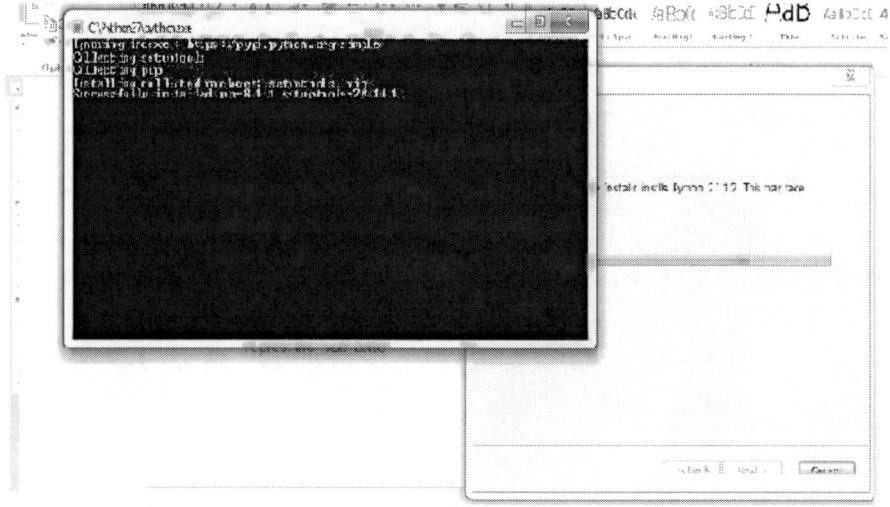

Your python has been installed in your computer and is now ready to use. Find it in drive C, or wherever you have saved it.

There can be glitches along the way, but there are options which are presented in this article. If you follow it well, there is no reason that you cannot perform this task.

It's important to note that there's no need to compile programs. Python is an interpretive language and can execute quickly your commands.

You can also download directly from the Python website, by selecting any of these versions – 3.5.2 or 2.7.12. and clicking 'download'. (For this book, 2.7.12 is used, in general, for easy discussions).

See image below:

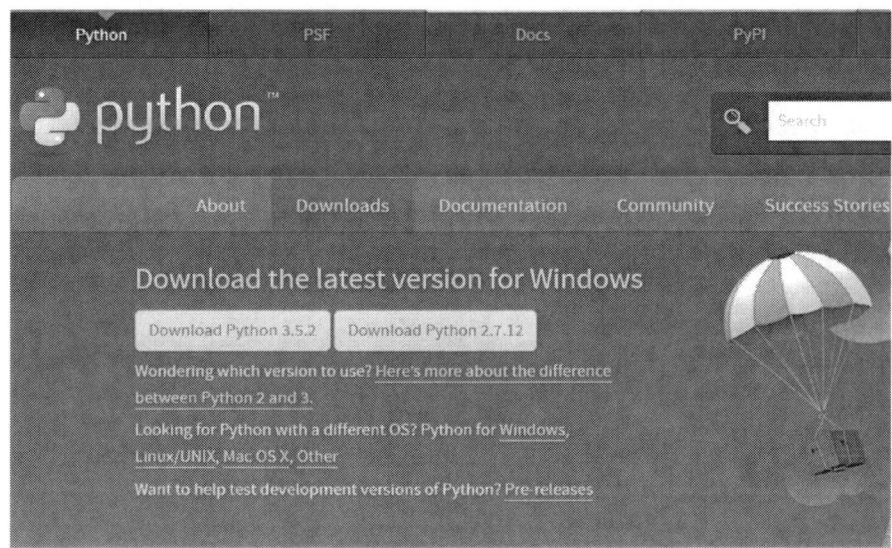

Follow the step by step instructions prompted by the program itself. Save and run the program in your computer.

For Mac

To download Python on Mac, you can follow a similar procedure, but this time, you will have to access the "Python.mpkg" file, to run the installer.

For Linux

For Linux, Python 2 and 3 may have been installed by default. Hence, check first your operating system. You can check if your device has already a Python program, by accessing your command prompt and entering this: python—version, or python3—version.

If Python is not installed in your Linux, the result "command not found" will be displayed. You may want to download both Python 2.7.12 and any of the versions of Python 3 for your

Linux. This is due to the fact that Linux can have more compatibility with Python 3.

For windows users, now that you have downloaded the program, you're ready to start.

And yes, congratulations! You can now begin working and having fun with your Python programming system.

Chapter 3: Basic Python Terms You Must Learn

As previously described, Python is a language used in computer programming. As such, you must be familiar with the most commonly used lingo to facilitate your understanding of the language. It's like learning the ABCs before you can read or write your first letters.

It's important to remember that there may be slight variations with the different Python versions. The example here is from version 2. So, here goes:

1. **Strings** – are the values enclosed inside double, single quotes, or triple quotes. They can be a word/text, or a group of words, or a Unicode, or other items.

   Example:

   mystring = 'welcome'

   mystring = "welcome"

   mystring = 'My little corner.'

   mystring = "My little corner."

   - The advantage of the double quotes is that you can include values within the double quotes.
   - The triple quotes signify long or lengthy strings. They are useful to avoid getting an EOL (End of the Line) error.

2. **Variables** – are containers for the strings. In the Python language, these are usually objects. These can be numbers or strings. Remember that you have to declare the variables, prior to using them.

   The numbers can be floating point numbers or integers.

   Use this syntax to define integers and floating point numbers. Integers are whole numbers, while floating point numbers are usually numbers with decimal points.

   Example:

   myint = 9

   myfloat = 9.0

   A more detailed explanation is presented in chapters 4 & 7.

3. **Statements** – are stated sentences or syntax used to call a function to compute, to write a value, or other procedures needed in executing or performing Python commands. There are several types of statements, which will be discussed in chapter 6 and other chapters of this book.

4. **Lists** – are just like your ordinary lists for items you want to create. They can contain any variable/s that you want to include in your list. They can be comparable to arrays. The variables are usually enclosed in brackets, and the items or values are separated by commas. The semi-colon can be used between lists. Lists are

immutable files – meaning they cannot be changed. More about this on the succeeding chapters.

The word-values are enclosed in single or double quotes, while numbers are not.

Example:

mylist1 = ['chemistry', 'anatomy', 2015, 2016];
mylist2 = [10, 20, 30, 40, 50];
mylist3 = ['grades', 'names', 'addresses']

When you add the function 'print' and press 'enter' or execute, this will appear:

Take note of the variations of colors that can identify the command or function (red colored word), from the variables (green), and from the results (blue colored words).

Examples of double quotes:

mystring4=["Vanessa Redgrave", "Tom Cruise", "Mel Gibson", "Matt Damon"]

5. **Loops** – are statements that can be performed or executed one after the other – repeatedly, or once. There are two general types of loops, the 'for' and the 'while' loops. Read more about loops in chapter 25.

6. **Function** – a piece of chord that executes some functions or logic. Examples are 'print', which prints your entry or variables; pow (power), which gets the answer for your numbers raised to a certain power. A specific example is this:

   To know the value of 8^9, you can use the Python function (pow). On your Python shell enter this statement:

   pow(8,9)

   When you press the 'enter' or the execute key, the answer will appear:

   In the specific example above, the answer is 134217728.

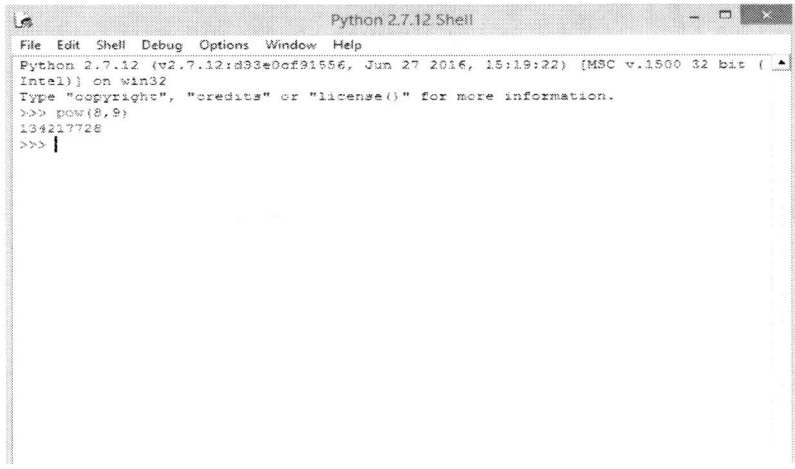

There are still various Python functions that will be discussed in the next chapters.

7. **Modules** – are files that contain various items, such as variables, definitions of functions, and executable statements, among others. Modules are used in cases when you want to save functions that you have created for easier accessibility later on.

This is because after using the Python interpreter, all the definitions, variables and functions you have created will be lost. Hence, you need to compile them in modules, so you can use them again, whenever necessary.

Python will automatically ask you to save your files, so you will never forget this function. Your modules should be saved with the name you assigned to them, and the suffix - .py.

21

It's best to assign names based on the object, or the purpose of your module. This way, you can recall the names of the modules easily.

8. **Shells** – are the blank boxes where you write your Python commands or statements.

9. **Tuples** – are similar to lists; they are immutable. You cannot change them. However, you can create new Tuples to modify the old ones. They can also be used as keys to dictionaries. Tuples will be discussed more in chapter 26.

10. **Classes** – are groups of related data, similar to strings, integers, and lists that use related functions. To introduce or identify a class, you can use the function word 'class'.

11. **Objects** – are used in Python language a great deal, because Python is object oriented. This means that the user can name his files according to what they are as a group, or as an individual value. An example is when a user names his data about Geography as 'Geo", or his research data on climate change, as 'climchange'.

12. **Concatenation** – a series of connected strings or variables use in Python programs. You can combine

small strings to become larger strings by utilizing the 'join'( ) procedure or the plus (+) sign.

There will be more Python terms that you will encounter as we proceed. Not all of them is included here.

But don't worry, the new terms will be defined as we use them in the succeeding chapters.

Chapter 4: Functions of the Python Standard Library

The Python standard library is one of the most extensive libraries in the world of programming. This is because it contains all the possible packages and modules that a programmer would need.

There are various reference materials, modules, significant built-in functions, and packaging tools to assist you in learning the Python language.

The common functions of a standard library are:

- It provides built-in modules that are easily accessible for programmers, who may encounter problems in creating and executing their codes.

- It acts as a guide to experts, who want prompt and reliable methods of creating and running their programs.

- It allows quick access to Python's system functionality and enhances programmer's output.

- It can also provide optional components essential to programming that comes from third parties.

In the Python standard library, an introduction is provided and then the essential materials follow. Here are some of the most basic contents of a Python standard library together with their specific functions.

1. **Built-in Functions** (types, constants and exceptions) - these are components that come

with the Python package. You can call in these functions when you need them, and when you need help in creating your statements.

These built-in functions are readily available to Python users:

Here are some of the most common functions:

- **abs( )** – this function is used when you want to determine the absolute value of a particular number.

```
>>>
>>> abs(35)
35
>>>
>>>
```

- **all( ), all(iterable)** - this function will return a 'True' result with a blank iterable, and if ALL the iterable (taken one after the other) are True. Refer to the chapter on loops for examples and actual use.

- **any( ), any(iterable)** – this will return a 'True' result, if ANY element of the iterable is true. A 'False' result is printed, when the iterable is left blank.

- **basestring( )** – this will determine if the object is a Unicode or a string.

- **cmp( )** – this is the key for comparing elements in a data. It is most useful in tuple.

- **dict( )** – this refers to the dictionary class.

- **dir([object])** – this refers to the directory. There are some examples in the chapters of this book.

Example:

If you want to access the built-in directory, use this statement:

dir(["__builtin__"])

press 'enter' or execute and the built-in directory will appear:

```
Python 2.7.12 Shell
File Edit Shell Debug Options Window Help
Python 2.7.12 (v2.7.12:d33e0cf91556, Jun 27 2016, 15:19:22) [MSC v.1500 32 bit (Intel)] on win32
Type "copyright", "credits" or "license()" for more information.
>>>
>>> dir(["__builtin__"])
['__add__', '__class__', '__contains__', '__delattr__', '__delitem__', '__delslice__', '__doc__', '__eq__', '__format__', '__ge__', '__getattribute__', '__getitem__', '__getslice__', '__gt__', '__hash__', '__iadd__', '__imul__', '__init__', '__iter__', '__le__', '__len__', '__lt__', '__mul__', '__ne__', '__new__', '__reduce__', '__reduce_ex__', '__repr__', '__reversed__', '__rmul__', '__setattr__', '__setitem__', '__setslice__', '__sizeof__', '__str__', '__subclasshook__', 'append', 'count', 'extend', 'index', 'insert', 'pop', 'remove', 'reverse', 'sort']
>>>
>>>
```

- **getattr( ), getattr(object, name[, default])** – this function is used in returning the value of the attributes of the specified object.

- **help( )** – this function is used in asking help from the Python's built-in functions and modules. It's interactive and can help you with a lot of things you would want to learn.

- **input( ), input([prompt]), raw_input( )** – the input data can help in accessing history features and similar data.

- **int( ), class int(x, base=10), class int(x=0)** - this function is used to return an integer. The types of the numeric may be a float, a complex number, a long number or an integer.

- **len(s)** – this will display the length of the items or elements of an object.

- **map( ) – (function, iterable,...)** – this function returns a list that provides a function applied to each iterable.

- **open( ), (object(name[,mode[,buffering])** – this keyword opens the data specified and returns the results.

  Where:

  name = name of file to be opened
  mode = this is a type of string that specifies how the file will be opened. The values are 'r'-reading, 'w'-writing, and 'a' for appending.

- **range(stop), range(start(,stop[step])** – this is a function that is commonly used in loops because of its arithmetic progressions. It returns a list of integers. The return defaults to (1), when the start argument is blank, and defaults to (0), when the step argument is omitted.

27

- **reload(module)** – this function will reload the module you want to access. The module should have been loaded previously and imported successfully, but be aware that there are some modules that may not reload, once they have been loaded previously. So, remember to save your modules.

- **round(number[,ndigits])** – this function rounds off numbers to the specified ndigits, after the decimal point.

- **vars([object])** – this returns the value of a __dict__attribute, and can function as the local dictionary.

Some of the other built-in functions are not mentioned in the above-mentioned list because they are used in the examples in some of the chapters.

The complex ones are also omitted to prevent information overload ('too much, too soon'). You might end up learning nothing because of the tremendous amount of data that can suffocate your brain, making it unable to assimilate anything.

It's better to learn some basic Python programming language. and be able to retain them than gobbling all the information at one time.

2. **String Services** – strings are crucial in Python programming, and a complete information about strings is provided in chapters 16 to 19 .

3. **Data Types** – there are various data types that you must become familiar with, if you want to

learn Python. These data types are sometimes handled differently.

4. **File and Directory Access** – You cannot access your files or data unless you know how.

5. **Numeric and Mathematical Modules** – Numerical computations are a part of the Python language. You can perform a number of data manipulations with these modules.

6. **Python (Runtime Services, Language and Interpreters, Compiler Package)** – the Python library is not complete without these packages. These are the programs that make Python work.

Anyway, you can access the built-in functions anytime you want; thus, you don't have to memorize all of them.

Below is an image of some of these built-in data in Python programming.

Name	Date modified	Type	Size
encodings	10/1/2016 10:03 AM	File folder	
ensurepip	9/30/2016 11:34 PM	File folder	
hotshot	10/1/2016 6:35 PM	File folder	
idlelib	10/9/2016 3:30 PM	File folder	
importlib	10/1/2016 12:02 AM	File folder	
json	9/30/2016 11:34 PM	File folder	
lib2to3	10/1/2016 6:35 PM	File folder	
lib-tk	10/1/2016 10:03 AM	File folder	
logging	9/30/2016 11:34 PM	File folder	
msilib	10/1/2016 6:35 PM	File folder	
multiprocessing	10/1/2016 6:35 PM	File folder	
pydoc_data	10/1/2016 6:35 PM	File folder	
site-packages	10/3/2016 3:25 PM	File folder	
sqlite3	10/1/2016 6:35 PM	File folder	
test	10/1/2016 6:35 PM	File folder	
unittest	10/1/2016 12:02 AM	File folder	
wsgiref	10/1/2016 6:35 PM	File folder	
xml	9/30/2016 11:34 PM	File folder	
__future__	6/25/2016 11:46 PM	Python File	5 KB
__future__	9/30/2016 11:34 PM	Compiled Python ...	5 KB

Aside from these, there are more optional services and modules that a user can utilize.

The Python programming language is extensive. If we were to discuss them all, it would take months to learn everything. So, let's choose the most significant parts that you can learn - given the circumstances.

Chapter 5: Basic Elements of Python

Learning the ABCs of anything in this world, is a must. Knowing the essentials is winning half the battle before you get started. It's easier to proceed when you are equipped with the fundamentals of what you are working on.

In the same manner that before you embark on the other aspects of python let us level off the basic elements first. You need to learn and understand the basics of python as a foundation in advancing to the more complicated components. This fundamental information will greatly help you as you go on and make the learning experience easier and enjoyable.

Familiarize yourself with the Python Official Website *https://www.python.org/.* Knowing well the website of python would give you the leverage in acquiring more information and scaling up your knowledge about python. Also, you can get the needed links for your work

Learn from Python collections. Locate python collections such as records, books, papers, files, documentations and archives and learn from it. You can pick up a number of lessons from these, and expand your knowledge about Python. There are also tutorials, communities and forums at your disposal.

Possess the SEO Basics. Acquire some education on Search Engine Optimization so you can interact with experts in the field and improve your python level of knowledge. That being said, here are the basic elements of Python.

Basic elements of Python Language and the programs

This is the phase where the program language is presented to make the user understand the type of language employed and knowing how to use it.

Interpretations and modules drafting

Python can be used as an active translator or transcriber by interaction through the web. It can also be employed to formulate lessons. In interaction, though, there is one serious concern: that is, it is impossible to keep a copy of what transpired. On the other hand, using lessons allows you to keep a record of the work done. In the interactive translator, you are allowed to open only one display page, while in lessons, you can open as many as you need.

Variables

Python uses information that are not constant, these are used to keep the data. When using these, be sure to put descriptions. These data could be names, age, addresses, gender and other similar material.

Outputs and Inputs

Any computer program requires interfacing between itself and the person using it. The user encodes and that is input, and the output is printing what has been encoded.

Mathematics

Numbers are the common language in computer programs including Python. Mathematical operations are used by Python as you will learn later on. Most of its language is represented by mathematical equations and symbols.

Loop

You need to understand the term loop in python. It is a symbol used to represent repeated word/s or sentence/s in python programming. Anything that is being repeatedly used can employ a loop.

Python categories

It is important to be acquainted with the types of python product categories for easy reference and understanding. Python categories are symbolized by A, B, C that signifies the shifts in language. Examples are 3.3.1 to 3.3.2. This means there are minor changes, but when it employs something like 2.xx to 3.xx it means there are major changes.

Cutting

This is a critical component of python which is used to copy the desired part of a data. It is a method of making programs simple by concentrating on items from a gamut of data. When you do that, you are actually removing components that are not relevant to the program.

Modules

Modules are files of descriptions and declarations of Python. It is a list of all the terminologies used by python with corresponding explanations of each. Python adopts a method of consolidating definitions into one folder called **module**. These modules can be introduced into different modules depending on the needs of the programmer or user.

This is created to allow users to have a better understanding and easy access to the standard library of Python. A programmer or even a beginner can make modules for his use.

Modules can be on: Indexing and searching, Audio and Music, Web development, Console and Database. Python provides an array of modules that you can use. You can also make your own.

Source codes

Generating Python source codes can be tedious, if you don't know how to derive your codes.

Program developers have now an application that converts your Python 2 codes to Python version 3 codes from AST.

You can create your own code as discussed in the chapters, and it's easy to append strings to a list to create a code, but it won't hurt you, if you know how to generate Python source codes. One way of doing this is to use context managers.

These are the most basic elements in python, there are more but with the ones presented, one can already start using python and learn the others, as you go on in your programming.

Chapter 6: Types of Python Statements

There are several types of Python statements that you must know. These statements will help you in creating your Python syntax/codes.

Here are the most common statements:

1. **Simple statements (simple_stmt)**

    These are statements that are composed of a single logical line. They may occur singly, or in several statements in one line. If there are several simple statements, they can be separated by a semicolon.

    The most common simple statement is the 'print' statement. You have also the 'delete' (del),'import', 'return', 'pass', 'continue', 'assignment', 'raise', 'break', to name some.

    Example:

    print var1

    This means that the values in variable 1 (var1) will be printed. Of course, var1 has to be defined first by assigning the values prior to executing the 'print' command. There will be examples in the next chapters.

35

2. **Assignment statements (assignment_stmt), (target), (target_list)**

    These statements are used when names are assigned to values, and when you want to modify mutable (can be changed) objects. The syntax is similar to that of the expression statements.

3. **Expression statements (expression_stmt)**

    These statements are generally used for computations and for evaluating an expression list. They are also useful in writing values. They usually return the (none) value, when used to call a procedure.

4. **import statements (import_stmt)**

    These are used to import files, functions or modules. Python has packages (directories) containing modules (files). You can quickly import modules by using the key 'import'.

    Example:

    I want to import my names1 and strings1 files; these are the statements:

    import names1

    import strings1

    See image below:

```
>>>
>>> import names1
('Potter Richard', 'Walker Henry', 'Fall Don', 'Dean James', 20, 34, 41, 32)




>>>
>>> import strings1
Remember.911
>>>
```

If Python cannot find the file, it will return the 'ImportError'. You cannot import your files if you have not saved them. Likewise, you cannot import a file or module that is not part of the Python program.

You can use importlib.import module( ), when you want to know more about the modules.

5. continue Statements (continue_stmt)

These statements indicate that the statement, usually a loop, continues with the next loop. It's used with the 'for' or 'while' loop.

Example:

for letter in 'Walker':

    if letter == 'W':

        continue

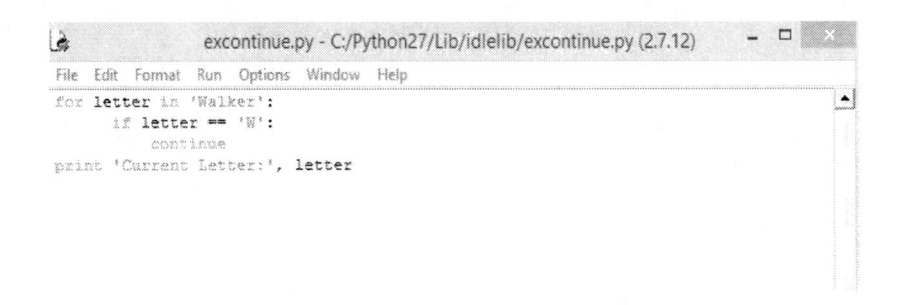

print 'Current Letter:', letter

```
for letter in 'Walker':
    if letter == 'W':
        continue
print 'Current Letter:', letter
```

When 'Run' and 'Run Module' are clicked. The result that will appear in a new shell will be the rest of the letters of "Walker".

```
Python 2.7.12 (v2.7.12:d33e0cf91556, Jun 27 2016, 15:19:22) [MSC v.1500 32 bit (Intel)] on win32
Type "copyright", "credits" or "license()" for more information.
>>> 
============== RESTART: C:/Python27/Lib/idlelib/excontinue.py ==============
Current Letter: r
>>> 
```

6. break statements (break_stmt)

These are statements that may occur in the 'for' or 'while' loops. Their function is to 'break' the nearest enclosing loop, and resumes execution on the next statement. But the loop will finally 'break' when the 'try' statement and the 'finally' clause are executed.

Example:

For letter in 'Walker':
   if letter == 'l':
      break
print 'Current Letter: ', letter

This 'break' statement will return these results:

Current Letter: W

Current Letter: a

This code will only return and print 'W' and 'a', which came before the break statement 'l'.

7. return Statements (return_stmt)

These statements are used usually in evaluating an expression list and exiting a function, operation or method. There are two forms the 'return' and 'return expressions'. They could be present in the definition of a function, but not in the definition of a nested class.

Example:

```
def doPrint():
    print "Clinical",
    return "Chemistry"
    print "is",
    return "interesting"

print doPrint()
```

See image below:

```
return.py - C:/Python27/Lib/idlelib/return.py (2.7.12)
File  Edit  Format  Run  Options  Window  Help
def doPrint():
    print "Clinical",
    return "Chemistry"
    print "is",
    return "interesting"

print doPrint()
```

When 'Run' is clicked, the results printed are only 'Clinical Chemistry', because after the 'return' statement, the function will stop, so it won't print/display the rest of the entries after the 'return' statement.

See image below:

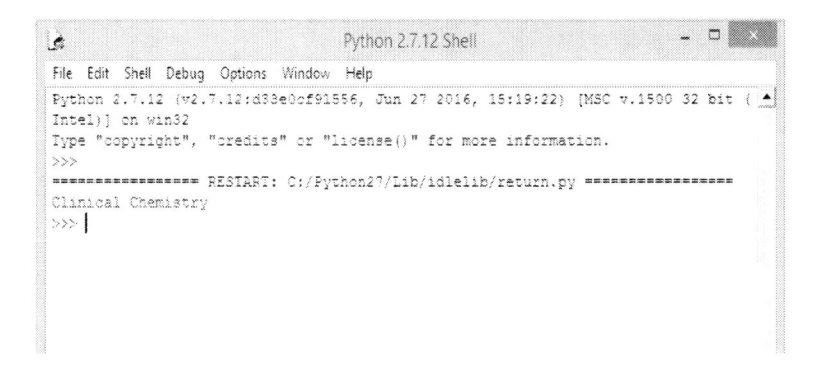

8. Else and Elif statements

These statements are discussed individually in chapters 23 and 24.

9. if Statements

These are statements that give an 'if' argument. It's often used with 'else' or 'elif' statements.

Example:

x= int(input("Please type a number: "))   # This is your base statement.

Please type a number: # This will appear, and you have

                                           to type a number.

                                           # the'if condition is:

41

```
if x > 0:

    x=0

print 'You have a good number!'
```

You have a good number!   #If the number you typed is higher than zero(0), This will appear in the results.

The entire Python statement will be like this:

```
x= int(input("Please type a number:  "))
    if x > 0:

        x=0

    print 'You have a good number!'
```

See image below:

When you click 'Run', and then 'Run Module', the result will be a statement asking you to type a number:

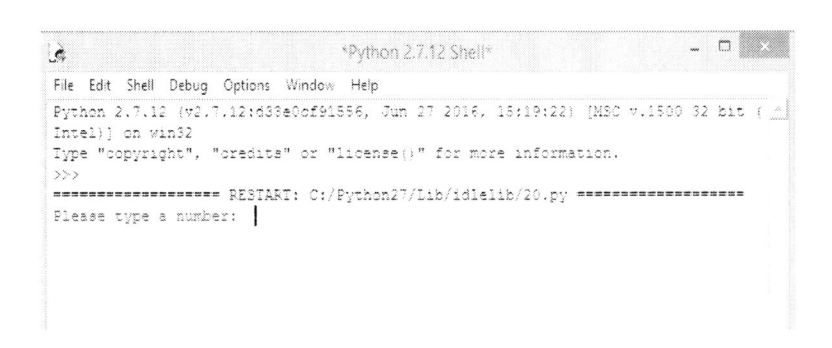

```
Python 2.7.12 (v2.7.12:d33e0cf91556, Jun 27 2016, 15:19:22) [MSC v.1500 32 bit (Intel)] on win32
Type "copyright", "credits" or "license()" for more information.
>>>
==================== RESTART: C:/Python27/Lib/idlelib/20.py ====================
Please type a number:
```

When you type 35, and press 'enter', this will be the result:

"You have a good number."

This is because this was the 'if' statement specified for values more than zero (0).

See image below:

43

```
Python 2.7.12 Shell
File Edit Shell Debug Options Window Help
Python 2.7.12 (v2.7.12:d33e0cf91556, Jun 27 2016, 15:19:22) [MSC v.1500 32 bit (
Intel)] on win32
Type "copyright", "credits" or "license()" for more information.
>>>
==================== RESTART: C:/Python27/Lib/idlelib/20.py ====================
Please type a number:  35
You have a good number!
>>>
>>>
```

There are still various statements used in Python, but for now, these are some of the essential types that are good to know.

Chapter 7: How to Start Using Python

Beginners may find it difficult to start using Python. It's a given and nothing's wrong about that. However, your desire to learn will make it easier for you to gradually become familiar with the language.

Here are the specific steps you can follow to start using Python.

Steps in using Python

Step #1 – Read all about Python.

Python has included a README information in your downloaded version. It's advisable to read it first, so you will learn more about the program.

You can start using your Python through the command box (black box), or you can go to your saved file and read first the README file by clicking it.

See image below:

This box will appear.

You can read the content completely, if you want to understand more what the program is all about, the file-setup, and similar information.

This is a long data that informs you of how to navigate and use Python. Also, Python welcomes new contributions for its further development.

You can copy paste the content of the box into a Window document for better presentation.

If you don't want to know all the other information about Python and you're raring to go, you can follow these next steps.

Step #2 – Start using Python.

First open the Python file you have saved in your computer. Click on Python as show below. In some versions, you just click 'python' for the shell to appear.

See image below:

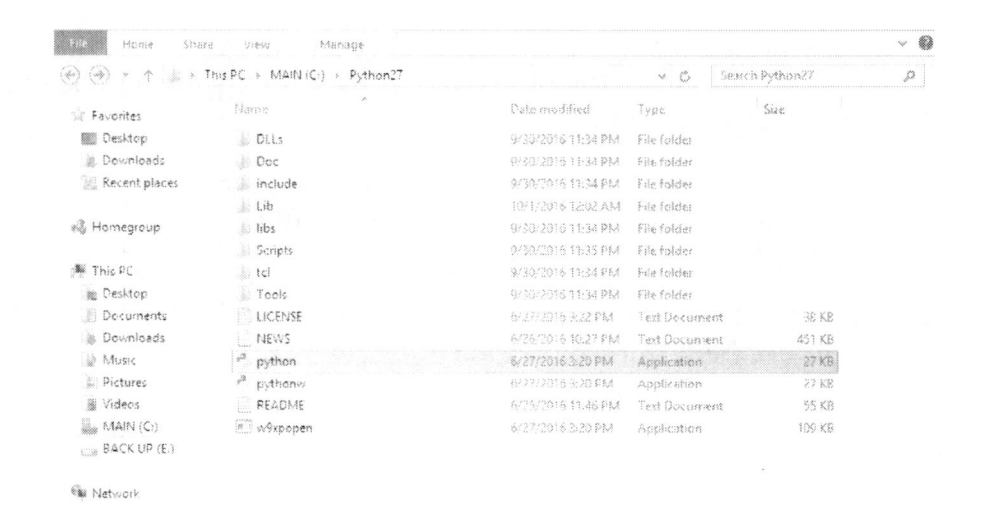

You can start using Python by utilizing the simplest function, which is 'print'. It's the simplest statement or directive of python. It prints a line or string that you specify.

For Python 2, print command may or may not be enclosed in parenthesis or brackets, while in Python 3 you have to enclose print with brackets.

Example for Python 2:

print "Welcome to My Corner."

Example for Python 3:

print ("Welcome to My Corner")

The image below shows what appears when you press 'enter'.

You may opt to use a Python shell through idle. If you do, this is how it would appear:

In the Python 3.5.2 version, the text colors are: function (purple), string (green) and the result (blue). (The string is composed of the words inside the bracket ("Welcome to My Corner"), while the function is the command word outside the bracket (print).

49

Take note that the image above is from the Python 2.7.12 version.

You have to use indentation for your Python statements/codes. The standard Python code uses four spaces. The indentations are used in place of braces or blocks.

In some programming languages, you usually use semi-colons at the end of the commands – in python, you don't need to add semi-colons at the end of the whole statement.

In Python, semi-colons are used in separating variables inside the brackets.

For version 3, click on your downloaded Python program and save the file in your computer. Then Click on IDLE (Integrated Development Environment), your shell will appear. You can now start using your Python. It's preferable to use idle, so that your codes can be interpreted directly by idle.

Alternative method to open a shell (for some versions).

An alternative method to use your Python is to open a shell through the following steps:

Step #1 – Open your menu.

After downloading and saving your Python program in your computer, open your menu and find your saved Python file. You may find it in the downloaded files of your computer or in the files where you saved it.

Step #2 – Access your Python file.

Open your saved Python file (Python 27) by double clicking it. The contents of Python 27 will appear. Instead of clicking on Python directly (as shown above), click on Lib instead. See image below.

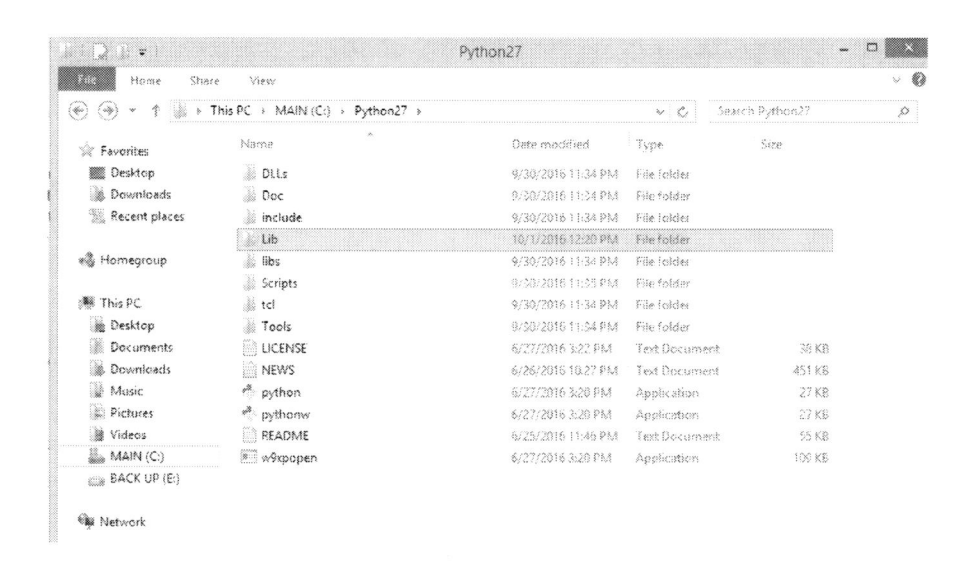

This will appear:

51

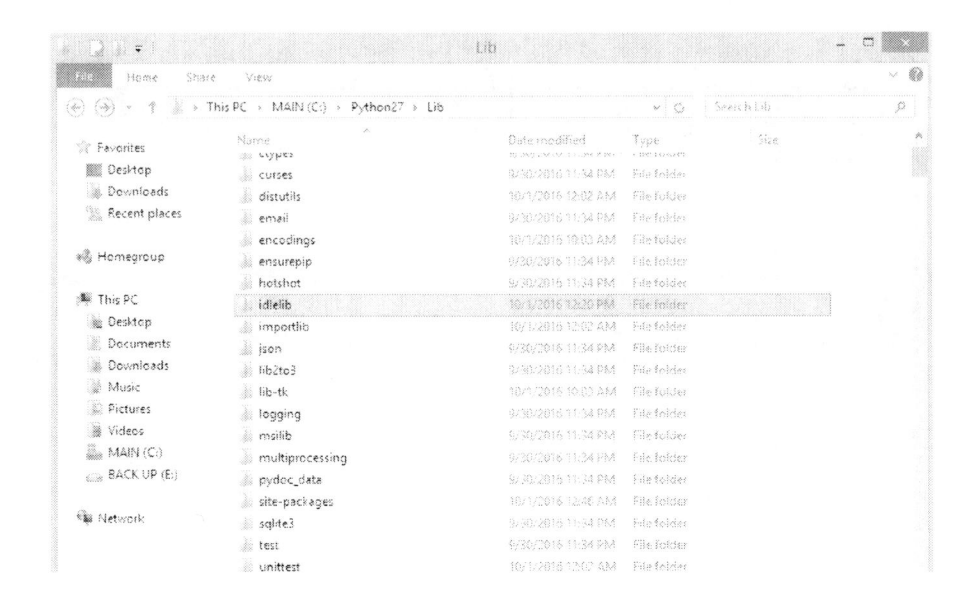

Step #3 – Click on 'idlelib'.

Clicking the 'idlelib' will show this content:

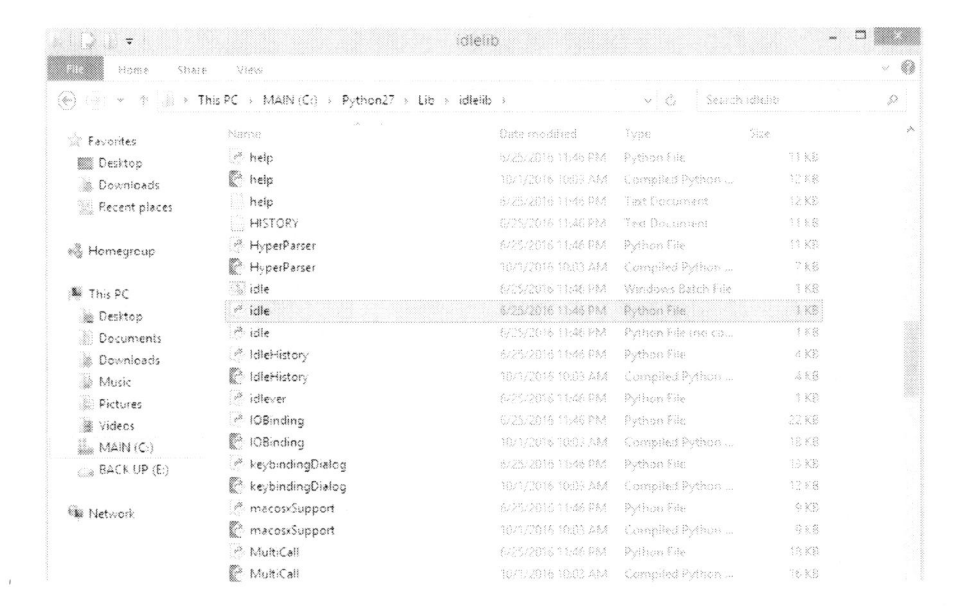

Step #4 – Click on idle to show the Python shell.

When you click on any of the 'idle' displayed on the menu, the 'white' shell will be displayed, as shown below:

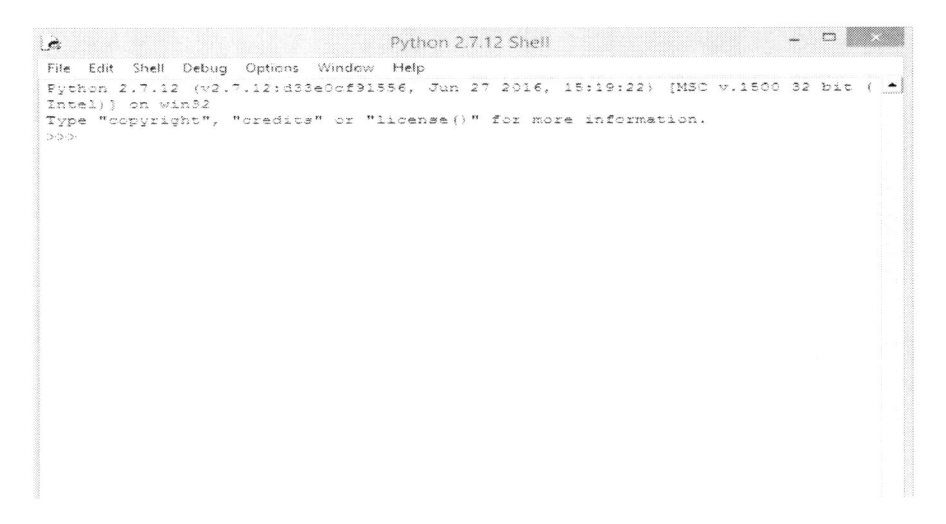

The differences between the three 'idle' menu, is that the first two 'idle' commands have the black box (shell) too, while the last 'idle' has only the 'white' box (shell). I prefer the third 'idle' because it's easy to use.

Step #5 – Start using your Python shell.

You can now start typing Python functions, using the shell above.

You may have noticed that there are various entries to the contents of each of the files that you have opened. You can

53

click and open all of them, as you progress in learning more about your Python programming.

Python is a programming language that has been studied by students for several days or months. Thus, what's presented in this book are the basics for beginners.

Chapter 8: Basic Python Syntax Rules

Every language has its syntax rules. Python is no different. For Python, there are essential rules that you have to remember. Applying them will help you a lot in using Python correctly.

1. **Python statements are delimited, when you create a new line.**

    When you create a new line, or press enter on your keyboard, the old line will be discontinued or delimited - unless you use the reverse slash (\ ), the brackets (curly { } and square [ ]) and parentheses ( ), to indicate that the statement has not ended yet.

    Example:

    print ('hello')

    When you type this on your Python shell and press 'enter', it's the end of the statement.

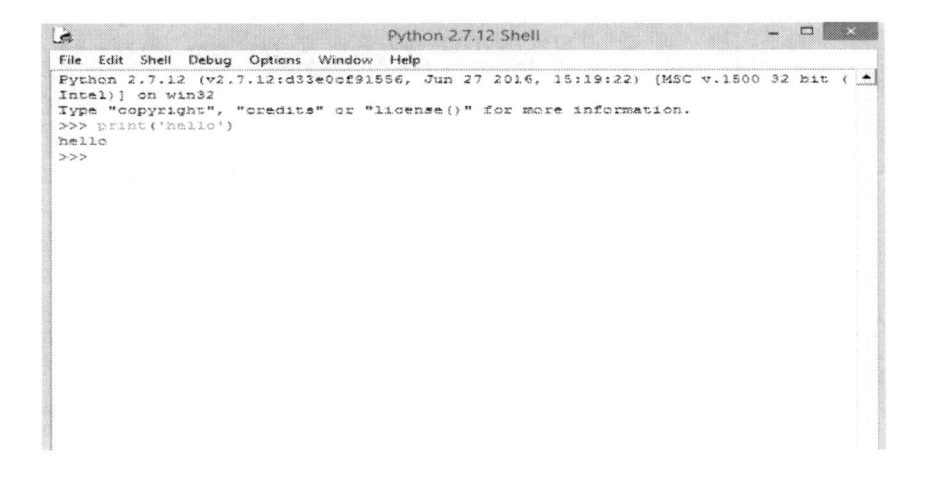

2. **Python statements, or variables in brackets, can span several lines, without using the continuation symbol (\ ).** But ascertain that commas are written in between each item.

   Variables or items enclosed with parentheses ( ), square brackets [ ], and curly brackets { } must be separated with commas, as well.

   Example #1:

   x = [2,

   [4,

   [6,

   [8]

   See image below:

```
*Python 2.7.12 Shell*
File  Edit  Shell  Debug  Options  Window  Help
Python 2.7.12 (v2.7.12:d33e0cf91556, Jun 27 2016, 15:19:22) [MSC v.1500 32 bit (
Intel)] on win32
Type "copyright", "credits" or "license()" for more information.
>>> print('hello')
hello
>>> x = [2,
         [4,
         [6,
         [8]
```

Example #2:

Mystring=['alpha', 'beta', 'gamma']

See image below:

```
Python 2.7.12 Shell
File  Edit  Shell  Debug  Options  Window  Help
Python 2.7.12 (v2.7.12:d33e0cf91556, Jun 27 2016, 15:19:22) [MSC v.1500 32 bit (
Intel)] on win32
Type "copyright", "credits" or "license()" for more information.
>>>
>>>
>>> mystring=['alpha', 'beta', 'gamma']
>>>
>>>
```

3. **Variables can be placed in a single line, but they must be separated by semi-colons.**

Example:

57

print ('names', 'grades'); print (10, 20, 30); print ('addresses')

See image below:

```
Python 2.7.12 Shell
File Edit Shell Debug Options Window Help
Python 2.7.12 (v2.7.12:d33e0cf91556, Jun 27 2016, 15:19:22) [MSC v.1500 32 bit (
Intel)] on win32
Type "copyright", "credits" or "license()" for more information.
>>> print('hello')
hello
>>> print('names','grades'); print(10,20,30); print('addresses')
('names', 'grades')
(10, 20, 30)
addresses
>>>
```

4. **When naming variables, use nouns in the lowercase.**

   Examples:

   names, patients, grades

   If you want to use two words, to be more specific, you can use an underscore.

   Examples:

names_patients

grades_students

Remember to enclose your variables using the single (''), or double quotes ("").

5. **When using functions, use a verb in the lowercase (small letters).**

   Examples:

   print, get, getarea

   When using two words, you can use an underscore to separate the two words.

   Example:

   get_area

6. **When using constant names, use a noun consisting of words using the uppercase, and separated by an underscore.**

   Example:

   MED_STUDENTS

7. **When using class names, the first letter of each word should be in the uppercase (capitalized).** This is called the camel-case.

    Examples:

    MyStudents

    MyStrings

    In some versions of Python, the first letter of the first word is expressed using the lowercase.

    Examples:

    myStudents

    myString

    Generally, Python is a case system program so take note of those items that make use of the lowercase (example: Python keywords), and those that make use of the uppercase as specified above.

8. **The Python body blocks should be properly indented** (generally 4 spaces – more or less - one-tab key in your keypad). This is a basic rule that you should apply when creating python syntax.

9. **When you want to continue to the next line, use the slash symbol (\).** This is to indicate that the next line is a continuation of the first.

    Example:

ave=element1 + \

element2 + \

element3

10. **Always use quotes to enclose your string literals (word-strings).** Python recognizes single quotes (' '), double quotes (" "), and triple quotes (""" """) – for multiple lines. These quotes identify word-strings.

Examples:

string1=['anatomy', 'chemistry', 'physiology', 'histology']

string2= ["anatomy", "chemistry", "physiology", "histology"]

string3 =["""This is the flash story I wrote for the website. It's made up of 300 words."""]

See image below:

61

11. **When creating multiple statements in a single line, remember to use a semi-colon (;).**

    Example:

    personnel = "Porky the Pig"; "Reed Avenue"; "College of Sciences";

    "Cheyenne Wyoming"

12. **When delimiting program blocks, use whitespaces or indentations.**

    Example:

    class EmployeeInfo:

        def __init__ (self) :

            print ("Employee Information Data.")

        def personalInfo(self, firstName, lastName) :

            self.firstName=firstName

            self.lastName=lastName

        def printPersonalInfo(self) :

            print(self.firstName, ' ', self.lastName, ' ')

Observe the indentations of the sample statement above. If you change the indentation, the result will give an error.

The Python code/statement above will be discussed in chapter 14 on the topic about "Class".

These are some of the basic rules in Python syntax. The other rules will be discussed as we go on with the other chapters.

Chapter 9: Application of Python in Math and Numbers

There are various types of numbers supported by Python; these are complex, integers (int), long integers, and floating point real values. Simple codes/statements are introduced to give you the basics.

Beginners may find it daunting to use Python in solving simple mathematical and number problems. People fear what they don't know. The truth, however, is that with a little addition of codes or signs, it's as easy as using your ordinary calculator. Here's how to do it.

Step #1 – Open your Python command box.

Open your saved Python file through your start menu. Click on 'python' for version 2, and the IDLE GUI to open your 'shell' for version 3. The downloaded versions can be the 2.7.12 and the 3.4.1 or the 3.5.2.

Step #2 – Solving addition, subtraction, multiplication and division problems

Let's say, you want to find the sum of 1,200 and 378. You just type 1200 + 378 and press 'enter'.

The answer will appear below your entry.

See succeeding image.

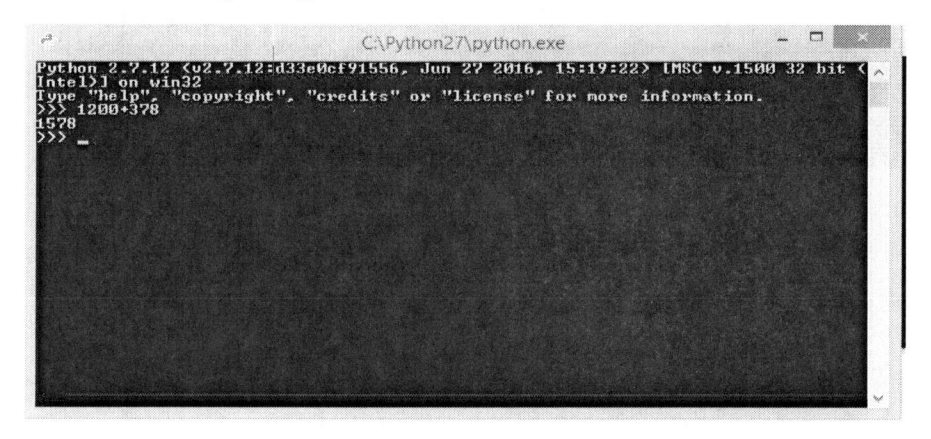

```
Python 2.7.12 (v2.7.12:d33e0cf91556, Jun 27 2016, 15:19:22) [MSC v.1500 32 bit (Intel)] on win32
Type "help", "copyright", "credits" or "license" for more information.
>>> 1200+378
1578
>>>
```

You can easily perform subtraction (-), addition (+), multiplication (*) and division (/), by using the specified signs.

Simply type the number and the sign and press 'enter'.

If you don't want your answers in fraction numbers in your division, you can use a double slash (//).

Example:

Divide 5.678/2 = 2.839 (with decimal points)

5.678//2 = 2.0 (whole number)

See image below:

Step #3 – Solving numbers with exponents

Exponents are the 'power' by which numbers are raised. For example, 10^9, means that 10 is multiplied by itself 9 times; 10 is the base and 9 is the exponent. It could also be read: 10 raised to the power of 9, or 10 raised to the 9th power.

Hence 10^9 = 1000000000

In Python, instead of multiplying 10, 9 times, you can use the double asterisk (**) as a short cut method.

Example:

10 ** 9 (enter the base number, and then the two asterisks and the exponent.)

See image below:

```
Python 2.7.12 (v2.7.12:d33e0cf91556, Jun 27 2016, 15:19:22) [MSC v.1500 32 bit (Intel)] on win32
Type "help", "copyright", "credits" or "license" for more information.
>>> 10**9
1000000000
>>>
```

More examples:

$4^6 = 4*4*4*4*4*4 = 4096$

This can be simplified by using two asterisks or stars.

4**6 = 4096

When you press enter, it will be giving the same answer. See image below.

67

Reminder:

In multiple signs, you must enclose (in parentheses), the solution that you want prioritized. Just like in your math problems, the chronological order of solving the problem is this: enclosed numbers are solved first, followed by exponents, then multiplication, then division, then addition and then subtraction.

Example:

$$5 + 6/5 + 2 - 7$$

If you want to prioritize the addition of 5 and 6, then enclose them in parentheses.

$$(5 + 6)/(5 + 5) - 7$$

In the problem above, (5 + 6) will be solved first, followed by (5+2), before 7 is subtracted.

Hence: 11/10 – 7 = - 5.9 or -6.

Notice that the answer will differ without the parentheses, so be sure to add them when needed.

5 + 6/ 5 + 2 – 7 = 1.2 or 1

If you didn't prioritize any numbers, your Python will compute the problem based on the universal mathematical rule, stated in the above-mentioned reminder.

See image below:

```
Python 2.7.12 (v2.7.12:d33e0cf91556, Jun 27 2016, 15:19:22) [MSC v.1500 32 bit (
Intel)] on win32
Type "help", "copyright", "credits" or "license" for more information.
>>> 4*4*4*4*4
4096
>>> 4**6
4096
>>> (5+6)/(5+2)-7
-6
>>> 5+6/5+2-7
1
>>>
```

If you want to find out the functions available for math, simply type 'import math' (without the quotes) and press 'enter'.

The word 'math' will appear and then right click it to search (scroll down or up) for the different built-in functions or command words. Select the value you want and click 'enter', to access it.

Chapter 10: Using Variables and Assigning Values

Python makes use of variables. As previously discussed, variables can contain a string of words, an integer (number) or other items. Hence, they act as containers.

Step #1 – Specify the value of your variable.

In the example below, the value of your variable is 50.

Example:

Let's say you want your variable to be 50, you can enter this in your Python.

    myVariable = 50

This is for the Python version 3. The first letter is in the lower case and the first letter of the next words are in the upper case. This is termed the 'camel case declaration'.

You must remember that Python is case sensitive, so use the upper case and lower case letters whenever necessary.

    myVariableTitle = 50

Step #2 – Press 'enter'.

After entering or assigning the value, you can press 'enter', and the value 50 will appear. This is your value.

You can make use of it in math operations to compute whatever you want to compute.

If your syntax is wrong, a syntax error appears in red ink, informing you of the mistake.

You can assign values to your variables by using the equal (=) sign. You have to name your variable before the equal sign and assign its values after the equal sign.

Examples:

>   name = "Billy"
>
>   surname = "Trump"
>
>   age = 45
>
>   height = 5

Your variables are: name, surname, age and height and the values assigned are: "Billy", "Trump", 45, and 5.

If you want to print your variables, you can create your statement or code this way:

>   name = "Billy"
>
>   surname = "Trump"

age = 45

height = 5

print name

print surname

print age

print height

See image below:

The original shell was used; thus, the variables are printed one by one by pressing your 'enter' tab/key.

Unlike if you open a 'New File', the results will be displayed all at once in a new shell:

```
>>> 
>>> name="Billy"
>>> surname="Trump"
>>> age=45
>>> height=5
>>> 
>>> print name
Billy
>>> print surname
Trump
>>> print age
45
>>> print height
5
```

If you decide to open a 'New File', the syntax/statement will appear this way:

73

```
name = "Billy"
surname = "Trump"
age = 45
height = 5

print name
print surname
print age
print height
```

When you click 'Run', and then 'Run Module', the results will appear in a new shell:

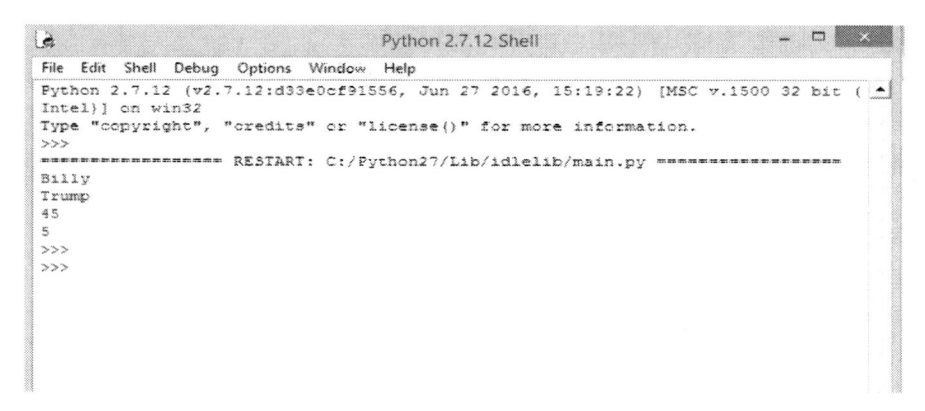

```
Billy
Trump
45
5
```

It's smart to name your variables according to their

objects/content, so you won't get confused accessing them later on.

As discussed, variables can contain names or integers, or different types of data. Just be sure to separate them with commas.

For variables that you want printed literally in a string, don't include them inside braces [ ]. These will appear in the final output.

Multiple assignments for variables

You can also assign, simultaneously, a single value to multiple variables. Here's an example:

Variables a, b, c, and d are all assigned to "1" memory location.

a=b=c=d=1

Another example is where variables are assigned individual values:

a, b, c, d, = 1, 2, "Potter", 3

The value of a=1

The value of b=2

The value of c = "Potter"

And the value of d = 1

Take note again, that numbers or integers are not enclosed in quotes (quotation marks – "), while word-strings are enclosed in single, double quotes, or triple quotes. (' ', or " ", or """ """).

Chapter 11: Learning the Built-in Modules and Functions

Python contains built-in modules and functions that come with the program when you download it into your computer. Downloading the Python versions 2 and 3 in the same computer may not work, because some of their contents/functions are incompatible with each other, although they are both from Python.

The following are quick steps in accessing and learning these built-in modules and functions:

Step #1 – On your shell, type help('modules) and press 'enter'.

This command or function will provide all the modules of Python available in your downloaded Python.

When you press 'enter', it will take a few seconds for the list of modules to appear.

```
Python 2.7.12 Shell
File  Edit  Shell  Debug  Options  Window  Help
Python 2.7.12 (v2.7.12:d33e0cf91556, Jun 27 2016, 15:19:22) [MSC v.1500 32 bit (
Intel)] on win32
Type "copyright", "credits" or "license()" for more information.
>>> help('modules')

Please wait a moment while I gather a list of all available modules...

AutoComplete          _md5                  ftplib                repr
AutoCompleteWindow    _msi                  functools             rexec
AutoExpand            _multibytecodec       future_builtins       rfc822
BaseHTTPServer        _multiprocessing      gc                    rlcompleter
Bastion               _osx_support          genericpath           robotparser
Bindings              _pyio                 getopt                rpc
CGIHTTPServer         _random               getpass               run
CallTipWindow         _sha                  gettext               runpy
CallTips              _sha256               glob                  sched
Canvas                _sha512               gzip                  select
ClassBrowser          _socket               hashlib               sets
CodeContext           _sqlite3              heapq                 setuptools
ColorDelegator        _sre                  help                  sgmllib
ConfigParser          _ssl                  hmac                  sha
Cookie                _strptime             hotshot               shelve
Debugger              _struct               htmlentitydefs        shlex
Delegator             _subprocess           htmllib               shutil
Dialog                _symtable             httplib               signal
DocXMLRPCServer       _testcapi             idle                  site
EditorWindow          _threading_local      idle_test             smtpd
FileDialog            _tkinter              idlelib               smtplib
FileList              _warnings             idlever               sndhdr
FixTk                 _weakref              ihooks                socket
```

Step #3 – Narrow down your search.

You can narrow down the search by being more specific. You can specify the type of module you want to find. Let's say, you want to access modules about 'profile', you can enter or type on your Python shell the following:

help("modules profile")

And then press 'enter'. The matching modules related to your designated search word will appear in your shell. See image below.

```
>>> help('modules profile')

Here is a list of matching modules.  Enter any module name to get more help.

_lsprof - Fast profiler
cProfile - Python interface for the 'lsprof' profiler.
hotshot - High-perfomance logging profiler, mostly written in C.
profile - Class for profiling Python code.
pstats - Class for printing reports on profiled python code.
test.profilee - Input for test_profile.py and test_cprofile.py.
test.test_cprofile - Test suite for the cProfile module.
test.test_profile - Test suite for the profile module.
test.test_sys_setprofile

>>>
```

The above image is only an example to demonstrate how to be more specific in your search for modules.

Step #4 – Find the built-in functions and modules.

You can access the Python built-in functions through your shell by typing the following:

> dir(['__builtin__'])

See image below:

```
>>>
>>> dir(['__builtin__'])
['__add__', '__class__', '__contains__', '__delattr__', '__delitem__', '__delsli
ce__', '__doc__', '__eq__', '__format__', '__ge__', '__getattribute__', '__getit
em__', '__getslice__', '__gt__', '__hash__', '__iadd__', '__imul__', '__init__',
'__iter__', '__le__', '__len__', '__lt__', '__mul__', '__ne__', '__new__', '__r
educe__', '__reduce_ex__', '__repr__', '__reversed__', '__rmul__', '__setattr__'
, '__setitem__', '__setslice__', '__sizeof__', '__str__', '__subclasshook__', 'a
ppend', 'count', 'extend', 'index', 'insert', 'pop', 'remove', 'reverse', 'sort'
]
>>>
```

The different functions will appear on your Python shell. You can choose any of the functions you want to use.

You can also access the built-in functions or modules by importing them. This is done by opening your idle shell, and then typing:

      import urllib

and then, type

      dir(urllib)

When you press 'enter', all the Python modules will be displayed on your shell.

See image below:

79

```
Python 2.7.12 Shell
File Edit Shell Debug Options Window Help
Python 2.7.12 (v2.7.12:d33e0cf91556, Jun 27 2016, 15:19:22) [MSC v.1500 32 bit (
Intel)] on win32
Type "copyright", "credits" or "license()" for more information.
>>> import urllib
>>> dir(urllib)
['ContentTooShortError', 'FancyURLopener', 'MAXFTPCACHE', 'URLopener', '__all__'
, '__builtins__', '__doc__', '__file__', '__name__', '__package__', '__version__
', '_asciire', '_ftperrors', '_have_ssl', '_hexdig', '_hextochr', '_hostprog', '
_is_unicode', '_localhost', '_noheaders', '_nportprog', '_passwdprog', '_portpro
g', '_queryprog', '_safe_map', '_safe_quoters', '_tagprog', '_thishost', '_typep
rog', '_urlopener', '_userprog', '_valueprog', 'addbase', 'addclosehook', 'addin
fo', 'addinfourl', 'always_safe', 'base64', 'basejoin', 'c', 'ftpcache', 'ftperr
ors', 'ftpwrapper', 'getproxies', 'getproxies_environment', 'getproxies_registry
', 'i', 'localhost', 'noheaders', 'os', 'pathname2url', 'proxy_bypass', 'proxy_b
ypass_environment', 'proxy_bypass_registry', 'quote', 'quote_plus', 're', 'repor
thook', 'socket', 'splitattr', 'splithost', 'splitnport', 'splitpasswd', 'splitp
ort', 'splitquery', 'splittag', 'splittype', 'splituser', 'splitvalue', 'ssl', '
string', 'sys', 'test1', 'thishost', 'time', 'toBytes', 'unquote', 'unquote_plus
', 'unwrap', 'url2pathname', 'urlcleanup', 'urlencode', 'urlopen', 'urlretrieve'
]
>>>
```

Step #5 – Find the uses of function words.

You can now explore the uses/functions of the function words displayed on your shell. That is, if you don't know the function of the word.

Let's say you want to learn more about the uses of the function word 'max', you can use the help function by entering the following command:

    help(max)

Press enter or execute. The use or functions of the word 'max' will be displayed on your shell, just like in the image below:

Based on the results in the image shown above, apparently, the function of 'max' is to show or display the largest item or largest (maximum) argument.

Therefore, if you want to know the largest item in a certain string, type max and then the values, and press enter.

The item with the highest value will be selected, just like the example below:

See image below:

81

As shown above, the highest value of the first set is 10, and the second is 11.

Step #5 - Access the Python modules and built-in functions from your downloaded file.

Another alternative is to access the different Python functions from the files that you have saved.

Remember, if your Python syntax or statement is wrong, the words will be colored red. So, it's easy to detect errors in your commands or statements.

Chapter 12: Creating, Saving and Running Python Files

You can create and save your Python files, so you can easily access and run them, whenever you need them. There are standard data types used in Python that you have to learn; these are: strings, lists, numbers, tuples and the dictionary.

But how do you create, save and run your own files?

Here's how:

Step #1 – Open your Python shell.

As instructed in the earlier chapter, after you have downloaded and saved the Python program in your computer/device, you can open your Python shell by clicking your saved Python and click IDLE (for Python version 3) or follow the instructions for version 2 as discussed in chapter 7.

Step #2 – Click on the 'File' menu of your shell.

At the left, uppermost portion of your Python shell, click the 'File' menu. The scroll down options will appear. Click on 'New File'. See image below:

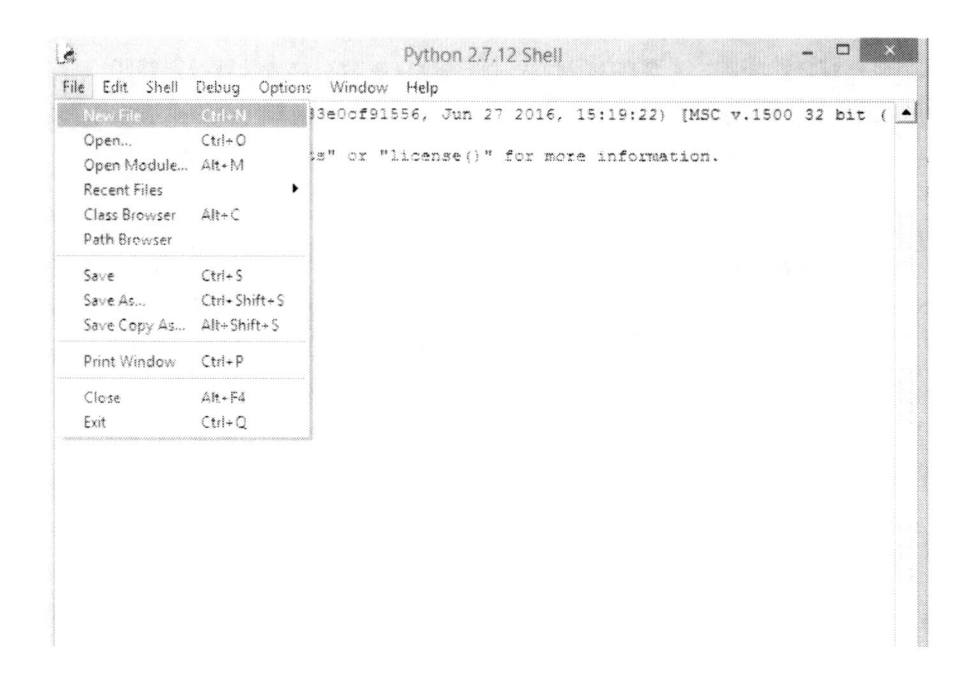

Step #3 – Create your 'New File'.

When you click on the 'New File' option, a blank box will appear. See image below:

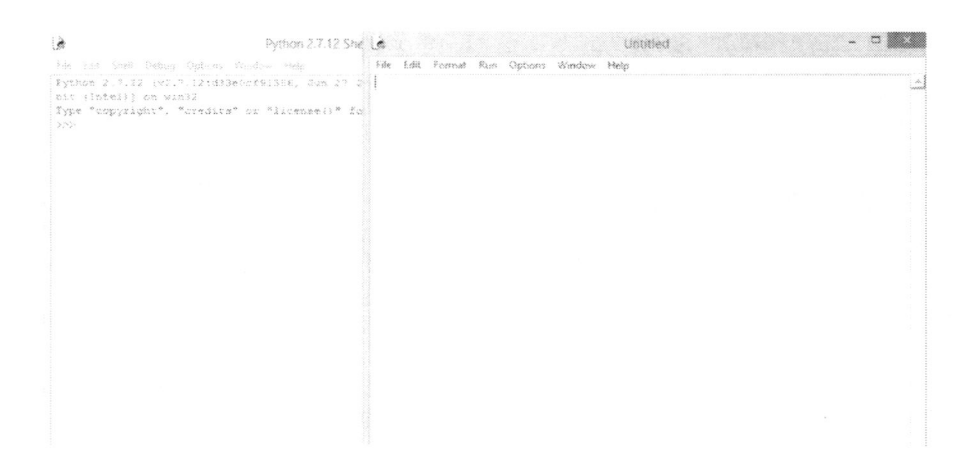

The new box is where you can create your file for saving. If you have noticed, the file is still untitled because you will be assigning the title before you can save it. You may save the file first before proceeding, or proceed to write your Python statement/code before saving.

Write your file.

For example, you want to create a file to provide the maximum or largest value of your variables (a, b, c, d), you can enter in your new file in the following manner:

    a=int(input("Please enter 1st number"))

    b=int(input("Please enter 2nd number"))

    c=int(input("Please enter 3rd number"))

    d=int(input("Please enter 4th number"))

    print (max(a,b,c,d))

See image below:

```
a=int(input("Please enter 1st number"))
b=int(input("Please enter 2nd number"))
c=int(input("Please enter 3rd number"))
d=int(input("Please enter 4th number"))

print (max(a,b,c,d))
```

Make sure you enter the correct items and had used the necessary quotes and parentheses.

Any error in the signs, indentations, and quotes in your statement will yield errors.

Python won't be able to execute your command, and says so in red ink.

Step #4 – Save your New File.

You can save your 'New File' before writing it. Just access the 'File' menu, and choose 'Save As'.

See image below:

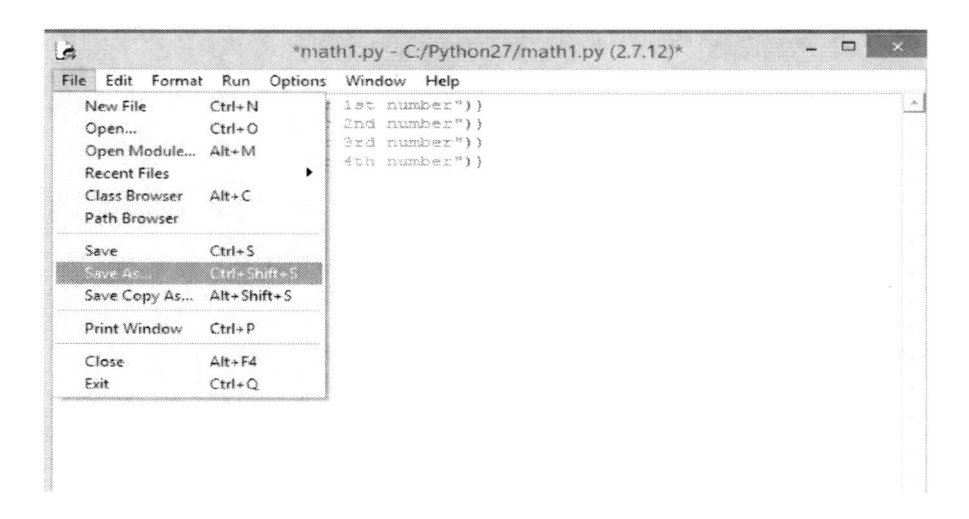

When you click on the 'Save As' option, a box will appear allowing you to select the name of your file, and where you want to save your file. Ascertain that your file is with the suffix .py.

Let's say you want to name your file math1. Type the name on the provided box, and press 'Save'. See image below:

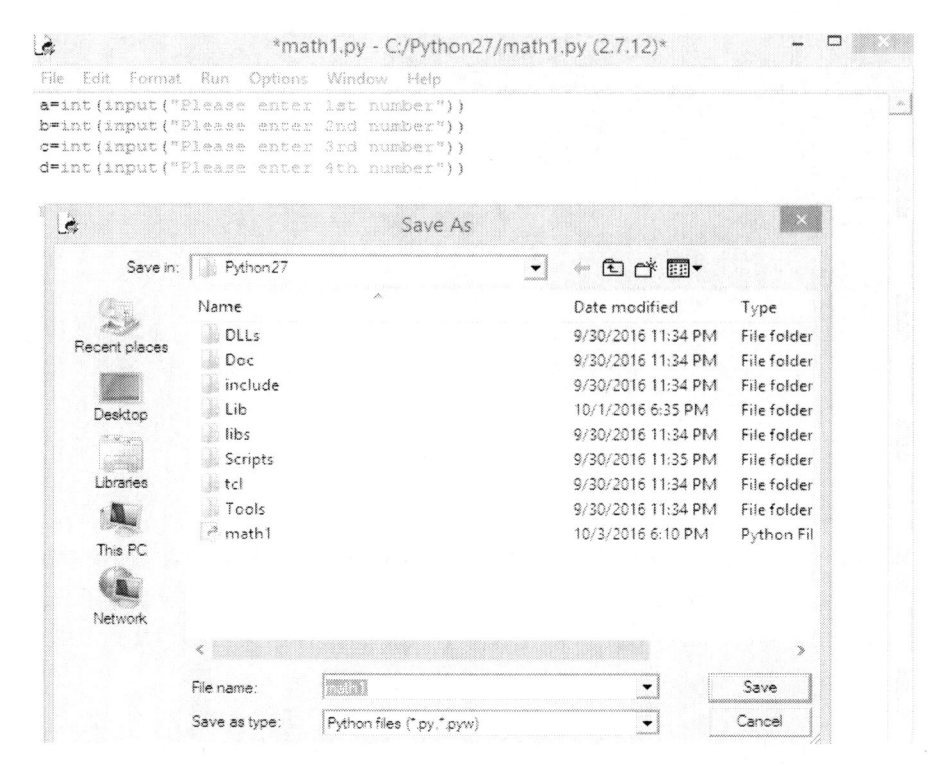

Step #5 – Run your 'New File' (math 1) or module.

You can now run your 'New File' by clicking on the 'Run' option, or key in F5 on your computer's keypads. See image below:

When you click on the 'Run Module' option, a new shell will appear. You can now enter your variables or values. See image below:

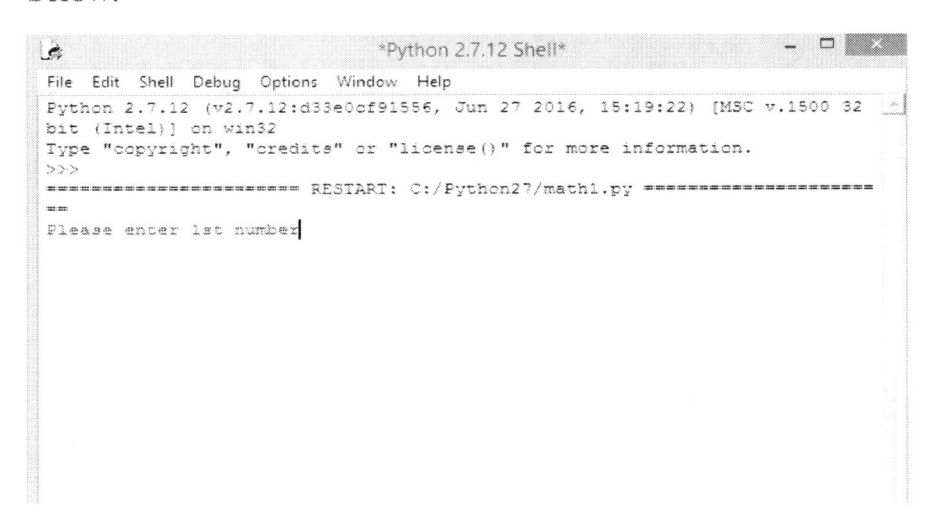

89

Test your file if it's working by providing the values required. Let's say the values of your items - a, b, c, and d - are 1356, 1827, 1359 and 1836. When you press 'enter', the value 1836 will appear, because it is the largest or highest value. See image below.

```
Python 2.7.12 (v2.7.12:d33e0cf91556, Jun 27 2016, 15:19:22) [MSC v.1500 32 bit (
Intel)] on win32
Type "copyright", "credits" or "license()" for more information.
>>>
======================= RESTART: C:/Python27/math1.py =======================
Please enter 1st number1356
Please enter 2nd number1827
Please enter 3rd number1359
Please enter 4th number1836
1836
>>>
>>> 
```

Of course, you can add more statements/codes, if you wish. This is just an example on how to create and save your Python file.

You can add another item/command, ("Please press enter to exit"), to provide easier access. Save your file again. See image below.

```
a=int(input("Please enter 1st number"))
b=int(input("Please enter 2nd number"))
c=int(input("Please enter 3rd number"))
d=int(input("Please enter 4th number"))

print (max(a,b,c,d))

input("Please press enter to exit")
```

Remember to ALWAYS save any changes you made in your Python statement, and double check that your saved file is a .py file.

Take note that Python doesn't compile your programs, you have to run them directly.

Deleting files

To delete files, use the key 'del'.

Example:

myname="Lincoln"

myage=20

del myname

This will delete your variable 'myname', and whatever is specified in your command or code.

You can delete as many variables as you want. Don't worry, you can always create new files, if you want to.

Chapter 13: Utilizing User-Defined Functions

User-defined functions often come to play when creating your Python codes. These functions can be used when you want a task or code done repeatedly. Functions can also help in maintaining your codes.

Keep in mind that you have also your built-in functions, which you can easily 'call', whenever you need them. However, you can create and utilize your own user-defined functions.

Step #1 – Use a keyword to define function.

The function should be defined first making use of the word 'def', and then the name of its function.

When you want to define a function, you can use the general code below:

>   def functionname (arg1, arg2, arg3)
>
>   statement1
>
>   statement2
>
>   statement3

Press 'enter' twice to access results.

Take note: arg stands for argument.

Example:

You are an employer, and you want to print the numbers (num) of your employees, thus, you defined 'employee' as the name of your file.

>   def employee(num)

print ("num")

See image below:

```
Python 2.7.12 (v2.7.12:d33e0cf91556, Jun 27 2016, 15:19:22) [MSC v.1500 32 bit ( 
Intel)] on win32
Type "copyright", "credits" or "license()" for more information.
>>>
>>> def employee(num) :
        print ('employee', num)
```

When you press enter, and input a number, the function will keep going until you decide to stop. So, the function can work repetitively. See image below:

```
Python 2.7.12 (v2.7.12:d33e0cf91556, Jun 27 2016, 15:19:22) [MSC v.1500 3: 
Intel)] on win32
Type "copyright", "credits" or "license()" for more information.
>>>
>>> def employee(num) :
        print ('employee', num)

>>> employee (101)
('employee', 101)
>>>
>>> employee (301)
('employee', 301)
```

You can also create the Python syntax this way:

def employee(num)

print 'employee', num

Press 'enter' twice and then you can begin entering the numbers. The program will print it ad infinitum. See image below:

```
Python 2.7.12 (v2.7.12:d33e0cf91556, Jun 27 2016, 15:19:22) [MSC v.1500 32 bit (
Intel)] on win32
Type "copyright", "credits" or "license()" for more information.
>>>
>>> def employee(num) :
        print 'employee', num

>>> employee (101)
employee 101
>>> employee (301)
employee 301
>>> employee (34)
employee 34
>>> employee (1)
employee 1
>>>
```

Functions can have no arguments, or have a couple of arguments. The arguments can be numbers, or strings.

You can also make use of the keyword 'return' to 'return' results (the 'return' key indicates that answers to the computation specified will be 'returned' – (displayed in the results).

Example:

If you want to obtain the average of the grades of students in 4 subjects, you can create the code this way: You can use this code for as long as you don't exit the shell. If you want to save it, you can create a New File so you could save it.

    def grades(a,b,c,d) :

        return ((a+b+c+d)/4)

See image below:

95

```
Python 2.7.12 Shell
File Edit Shell Debug Options Window Help
Python 2.7.12 (v2.7.12:d33e0cf91556, Jun 27 2016, 15:19:22) [MSC v.1500 32 bit (
Intel)] on win32
Type "copyright", "credits" or "license()" for more information.
>>>
>>> def grades(a,b,c,d) :
        return ((a+b+c+d)/4)

>>>
```

When you, or the student enters his grades following the syntax/statement, the 'return' results would be the computed value already. See image below:

```
Python 2.7.12 Shell
File Edit Shell Debug Options Window Help
Python 2.7.12 (v2.7.12:d33e0cf91556, Jun 27 2016, 15:19:22) [MSC v.15
Intel)] on win32
Type "copyright", "credits" or "license()" for more information.
>>>
>>> def grades(a,b,c,d) :
        return ((a+b+c+d)/4)

>>>
>>> grades(80,79,81,84)
81
>>> grades(77,85,87,77)
81
>>> grades(90,88,86,85)
87
>>> grades(88,80,79,85)
83
>>> |
```

The student has to type in the shell, after the arrows (>>>), following the given format:

grades(80,90,85,75)

Through this method, you can compute the grades of your students- ad infinitum.

Take note that 'return' results are different from 'return' statements. Refer to the chapter involved.

Keep in mind that you have first to define (def) the function, before your code can work, and print the results.

Remember to add the colon (:) after your def statement. You must also separate the arguments by commas.

In default parameters, the originally assigned value is printed, when the user doesn't enter any value.

In multiple parameters, an asterisk (*) can be used to indicate this.

Be adventurous and discover the joy of knowing how to make your codes work with Python.

Chapter 14: How to Use and Define a Class

Classes, as defined earlier, are data that contain objects that are related to each other. The functions that are applied to these classes are also related to each other.

The keyword 'self' is a sparring partner for class data because it's used in creating your class statements.

For classes to be used correctly, it's important to create correct Python statements and syntax.

How do use your classes? Here's how.

For example, you're the 'big boss' of a company, and you want to compile the personal information of your employees, you can create a Python class code to do this.

Step #1 – Use the 'class' keyword.

Open a New File and save it. Use the 'class' keyword in introducing your class code.

Step #2 – Add the name of your 'class'.

Add the name of your class (file name). Since the data is the personal information of your employees, you may want to name it - PersonnelInfo .

Step #3 – Add the colon at the end of the first statement.

Hence, it will appear this way: class PersonnelInfo :

Step #4 – Define your variables

You have to define or assign variables to your data. You need to use the word 'self' to indicate that the code is referring to the class.

In general, a class statement appears this way:

class ClassName :

<statement-1>

.

.

.

<statement – last>

Step #5 – Run your module.

See image below:

e

```
classcode.py - C:/Python27/Lib/idlelib/classcode.py (2.7.12)
File  Edit  Format  Run  Options  Window  Help
class Employee    Python Shell
    def person                        e, lastName) :
        self.f    Check Module  Alt+X
        self.l    Run Module    F5
    def printPersonalInfo(self) :
        print(self.firstName, " ", self.lastName, " ")

employeeName=EmployeeInfo ()
employeeName.personalInfo("Virginia", "Walker")
employeeName.printPersonalInfo()
```

Two types of class object operations

1. **Class instantiation** – this type utilizes function notations in calling a class object. A special method, (double underscore)__init__(double underscore) ( ) (bracket), can be defined by a class. __init__is called a class constructor and it's used to initialize (init) a value. Python uses this keyword to indicate (initialization).

   Example:

   def __init__self :

   self.data = [ ]

99

The class instantiation using the __init__ ( ) method, automatically raises __init__( ) for the newly formed class instance.

Example:

class EmployeeInfo:

   def __init__ (self) :

      print ("Employee Information Data")

      def personalInfo(self, firstName, lastName) :

      self.firstName=firstName

      self.lastName=lastName

   def printPersonalInfo(self) :

      print(self.firstName, " ", self.lastName, " ")

employeeName=EmployeeInfo ()

employeeName.personalInfo("Virginia", "Walker")

employeeName.printPersonalInfo()

See image below:

```
class EmployeeInfo:
    def __init__(self) :
        print ("Employee Information Data.")
    def personalInfo(self, firstName, lastName) :
        self.firstName=firstName
        self.lastName=lastName
    def printPersonalInfo(self) :
        print(self.firstName, ' ', self.lastName, ' ')

employeeName=EmployeeInfo ()
employeeName.personalInfo('Virginia', 'Walker')
employeeName.printPersonalInfo()
```

Save and click 'Run', and then 'Run Module'.

When you click 'Run Module', a new shell will be opened with this image:

101

```
Python 2.7.12 Shell
File Edit Shell Debug Options Window Help
Python 2.7.12 (v2.7.12:d33e0cf91556, Jun 27 2016, 15:19:22) [MSC v.1500 32 bit (
Intel)] on win32
Type "copyright", "credits" or "license()" for more information.
>>>
================ RESTART: C:/Python27/Lib/idlelib/classcode.py ================
Employee Information Data.
('Virginia', ' ', 'Walker', ' ')
>>>
```

You can now enter your employees' names. See image below.

```
Python 2.7.12 Shell
File Edit Shell Debug Options Window Help
Python 2.7.12 (v2.7.12:d33e0cf91556, Jun 27 2016, 15:19:22) [MSC v.1500 32 bit (
Intel)] on win32
Type "copyright", "credits" or "license()" for more information.
>>>
================ RESTART: C:/Python27/Lib/idlelib/classcode.py ================
Employee Information Data.
('Virginia', ' ', 'Walker', ' ')
>>> 'Donnie, Tell'
'Donnie, Tell'
>>> 'Venus', 'Potter'
('Venus', 'Potter')
>>> ('Miriam', 'Wells')
('Miriam', 'Wells')
>>>
```

We have also what we call 'destructors' represented by the Python keyword __del__( ): (double underscore + del + double underscore + brackets + colon.

This function will destroy or delete specified data or acts as a trash can for the data. Just like __init__, it automatically functions even without 'calling' it out.

Example: (We'll use the same example above, but with the __del__ function.)

```
class EmployeeInfo:
    def __init__ (self) :
        print ("Employee Information Data.")
    def __del__ (self) :
        print ("Employee Information Data is discontinued")
    def personalInfo(self, firstName, lastName) :
        self.firstName=firstName
        self.lastName=lastName
    def printPersonalInfo(self) :
        print(self.firstName, ' ', self.lastName, ' ')


employeeName=EmployeeInfo ( )
employeeName.personalInfo('Virginia', 'Walker')
employeeName.printPersonalInfo( )
```

See image below:

```
class EmployeeInfo:
    def __init__ (self) :
        print ("Employee Information Data.")
    def __del__ (self) :
        print ("Employee Information Data is discontinued")
    def personalInfo(self, firstName, lastName) :
        self.firstName=firstName
        self.lastName=lastName
    def printPersonalInfo(self) :
        print(self.firstName, ' ', self.lastName, ' ')

employeeName=EmployeeInfo ()
employeeName.personalInfo('Virginia', 'Walker')
employeeName.printPersonalInfo()
```

If you use the del keyword in the object or instance, for example:

Adding employeeName.__del__ ( )

The resources or employees' name will be deleted or destroyed.

See image below:

```
class employeeInfo:
    def __init__ (self) :
        print ("Employee Information Data.")
    def __del__ (self) :
        print ("Employee Information Data is discontinued")
    def personalInfo(self, firstName, lastName) :
        self.firstName=firstName
        self.lastName=lastName
    def printPersonalInfo(self) :
        print(self.firstName, ' ', self.lastName, ' ')

employeeName=EmployeeInfo ()
employeeName.personalInfo('Virginia', 'Walker')
employeeName.printPersonalInfo()
employeeName.__del__()
```

When you click 'Run', and then 'Run Module', a new shell will open. See image below:

Example #2: (for __init__)

class Employee :

    def __init__ (self, name, address) :

        self.name=name

        self.address=address

print (employee.name)

print (employee.address)

See image below:

105

When you click 'Run', and then 'Run Module', another Python shell will open, printing the results. See image below:

```
Python 2.7.12 Shell
File Edit Shell Debug Options Window Help
Python 2.7.12 (v2.7.12:d33e0cf91556, Jun 27 2016, 15:19:22) [MSC v.1500 32 bit (
Intel)] on win32
Type "copyright", "credits" or "license()" for more information.
>>>
========================= RESTART: C:/Python27/init1.py =========================
Virginia Walker
Apt. G, Reed Avenue, Cheyenne, Wyoming
>>>
```

You can edit your code to produce results that are in congruence with your preferences. Isn't it fun?

Reminders:

For each definition, a colon (:) is added at the end of the statement.

'self' is always included in each member function, even if there are no arguments. Example of arguments are those values found inside the parentheses (self, firstName, LastName).

Double quotes or single quotes can be used with the arguments.

The constructor and destructor can contain arguments other than self. You can include any arguments you want. Example of arguments are (self, firstName, lastName). Make sure though that your __init__ arguments are included in the instances or objects' statements that come after the 'def'.

2. **Attribute references** – this type uses the 'object.name' of common Python syntax. Whenever you define a function of a class always pass an argument on 'self'. This is because the 'self' is pointing to the class.

Example:

We will be using the same code above – without the __init__ function. If you want the data about your employees, you can create your code this way:

```
class EmployeeInfo:
    def personalInfo(self, firstName, lastName) :
        self.firstName=firstName
        self.lastName=lastName
    def printPersonalInfo(self) :
        print(self.firstName, " ", self.lastName, " ")

employeeName=EmployeeInfo ()
employeeName.personalInfo("Virginia", "Walker")
employeeName.printPersonalInfo()
```

See image below:

```
class EmployeeInfo:
    def personalInfo(self, firstName, lastName) :
        self.firstName=firstName
        self.lastName=lastName
    def printPersonalInfo(self) :
        print(self.firstName, " ", self.lastName, " ")

employeeName=EmployeeInfo ()
employeeName.personalInfo("Virginia", "Walker")
employeeName.printPersonalInfo()
```

In the example above, in each definition (def) of a class, 'self' is always added for every function of the class. Notice also the indentations for the 'def' statements.

The following entries are not indented because the statements are not part of the definition of the class, but they are objects, or instances of the class.

  employeeName=EmployeeInfo ( )

  employeeName.personalInfo("Virginia", "Walker")

  employeeName.printPersonalInfo ( )

If you run the class code above, this would appear in your Python shell:

Tweak the codes and see what happens. Curiosity doesn't always kill the cat.

Chapter 15: Creating & Accessing Your Python Dictionary

Python dictionaries are usually enclosed by curly brackets { }. However, when accessing and assigning values, square brackets [ ] are used.

If you want to create your own dictionary, you can start with the key 'dict':

>   dict{ }
>
>   dict ['filename'] = ['values']

Example:

>   dict{ }
>
>   dict['name'] = "My name is Billy."

When you print this by running the module with this function:

>   print dict['name']

```
dict = {}
dict['name'] = "My name is Billy."

print dict['name']
```

The results will appear in a new shell/box – all the values of your dict['name'] will be printed.

See image below:

```
Python 2.7.12 Shell
File  Edit  Shell  Debug  Options  Window  Help
Python 2.7.12 (v2.7.12:d33e0cf91556, Jun 27 2016, 15:19:22) [MSC v.1500 32 bit (
Intel)] on win32
Type "copyright", "credits" or "license()" for more information.
>>>
================ RESTART: C:/Python27/Lib/idlelib/dict1.py ================
My name is Billy.
>>>
>>> |
```

You could also assign numbers as your dictionary's name, such as dict[1], and so forth. Make sure you have assigned values to your dictionary file.

Example:

dict[1] = "My age is 25."

You can print your dict[1], by using: print dict[1], to display its values/content. See image below:

```
dict1.py - C:/Python27/Lib/idlelib/dict1.py (2.7.12)
File  Edit  Format  Run  Options  Window  Help
dict = {}
dict[1] = "My age is 25."

print dict[1]
```

111

When you run the module, this will be the result:

```
Python 2.7.12 Shell
File Edit Shell Debug Options Window Help
Python 2.7.12 (v2.7.12:d33e0cf91556, Jun 27 2016, 15:19:22) [MSC v.1500 32 bit (
Intel)] on win32
Type "copyright", "credits" or "license()" for more information.
>>>
================ RESTART: C:/Python27/Lib/idlelib/dict1.py ================
My age is 25.
>>>
>>>
>>>
```

Notice that all the values of dict1 have been printed in the results.

If you want to print the complete dictionary, you can use this statement:

>   print tinydict

But there should be values assigned to your tinydict, or your results will show errors.

See image below:

```
tinydict.py - C:/Python27/Lib/idlelib/tinydict.py (2.7.12)
File Edit Format Run Options Window Help
dict = {}
tinydict={'student': 'Ted', 'grade': 86, 'college': 'engineering'}

print tinydict
```

After you click 'Run', and then 'Run Module', a new shell will appear with results like the image below:

```
Python 2.7.12 (v2.7.12:d33e0cf91556, Jun 27 2016, 15:19:22) [MSC v.1500 32 bit ( 
Intel)] on win32
Type "copyright", "credits" or "license()" for more information.
>>> 
================= RESTART: C:/Python27/Lib/idlelib/tinydict.py =================
{'grade': 86, 'college': 'engineering', 'student': 'Ted'}
>>>
>>>
```

You can also print all the values of your tinydict, by using this statement or code:

    print tinydict.values()

The results below will appear:

```
>>>
>>> print tinydict.values()
[86, 'engineering', 'Ted']
>>>
>>>
>>> |
```

Notice that there are >>> symbols in this shell. This is because the original shell was used without opening a 'New File'.

If you want to print the keys of your tinydict, you can use this statement:

    print tinydict.keys()

113

```
>>>
>>>
>>> print tinydict.keys()
```

When you press 'enter' or execute, the results will be this:

```
>>>
>>> print tinydict.keys()
['grade', 'college', 'student']
>>>
>>>
>>>
```

All the keys are printed in the results. Often, the results don't come in the order that it was presented/written in the tinydict.

Reminder:

If you have opted to create a 'New File', click the 'Run', and the 'Run Module'. If not, just press 'enter' and the results will be printed promptly in the same Python shell.

The advantage of creating a 'New File', however, is that you can edit the file without difficulty. This is because when you press the 'enter' key it does not execute the code, not until you click the 'Run' and 'Run Module' menu on the New File's shell, itself.

Accessing Values from a Python Dictionary:

You can access values from a Python dictionary by entering the correct code. To access values, you can use the square brackets and the keyword (key).

In the dictionary, the keyword is separated from its value by a colon (:), and the values are separated by commas, and all items are enclosed in curly braces { }.

Example:

    dict={'student': 'White', 'gender': 'female'}

    print "dict['student']: ", dict['student']

    print "dict['gender']; ", dict['gender']

See image below:

```
dict={'student':'White', 'gender':'female'}
print "dict['student']: " , dict['student']
print "dict['gender']: " , dict['gender']
```

Before you can access this though, the file should have been saved in your device.

Chapter 16: Creating and Combining Strings

Writing your strings properly for your codes can help you significantly in obtaining correct results.

These are the steps:

Step #1 – Open a 'New File'.

From your shell, open a 'New File', as instructed in the previous chapter. On this box, you can now create your string.

As previously defined, strings can contain variable numbers or words.

Step #2 – Identify your variables.

Let's say you have chosen three variables, a, b, and c. You can then assign a string to each of the variables before printing them.

Example:

    a=('This is a single quoted string.')

    b=("This is a double quoted string.")

    c=("""This is a triple quoted string.""")

    print (a)

    print (b)

    print (c)

See the example of composing and assigning values to your variables, using strings, demonstrated in the image below:

Step #3 – Save your New File.

Again, name and 'Save As' your 'New File' where you want it to be. In this case, the file is named string1 and saved in the Python file. Remember to save every time you make changes. See image below.

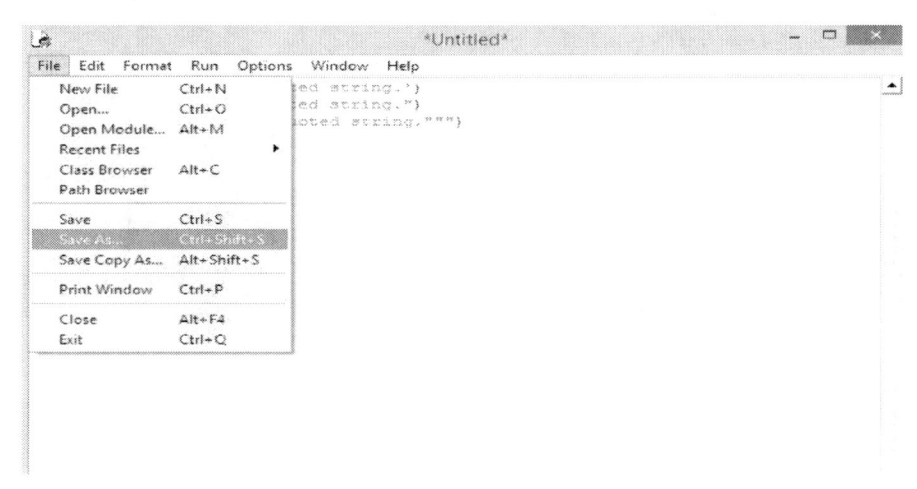

117

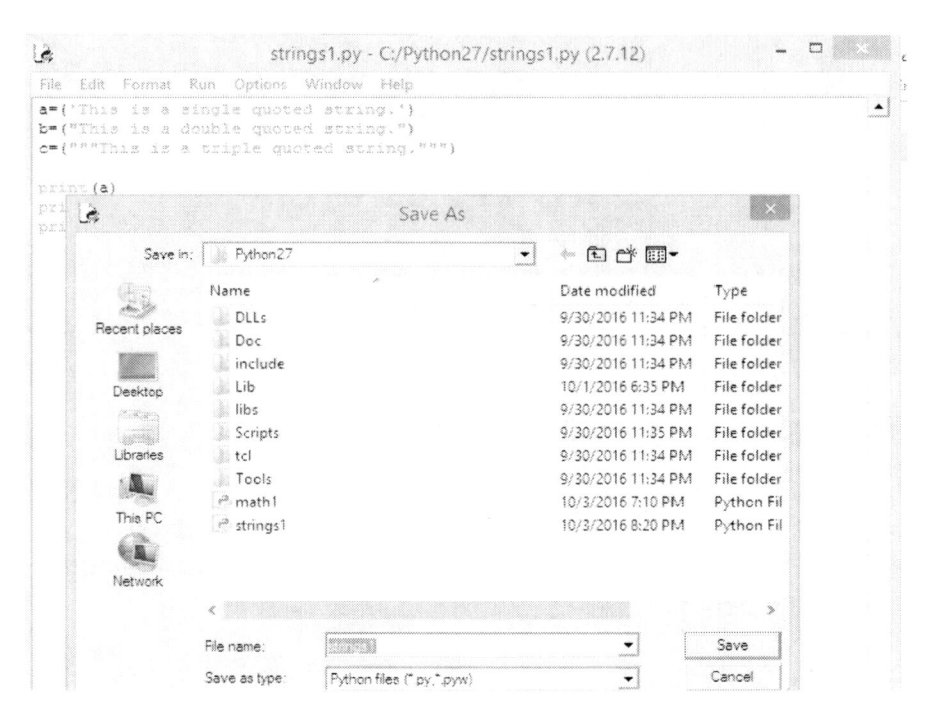

Step #4 – Run your 'New File'.

You can now run your new Python file by clicking 'Run" and then 'Run Module', or simply key in F5. See image below:

Step #5 – Use your new module (strings 1)

Go back to your Python shell and import your 'New File', strings1, so you can use it. Simply type: import strings1, and then press 'enter'. The results will appear, with your strings displayed quickly.

```
Python 2.7.12 Shell
File Edit Shell Debug Options Window Help
Python 2.7.12 (v2.7.12:d33e0cf91556, Jun 27 2016, 15:19:22) [MSC v.1500 32 bit (
Intel)] on win32
Type "copyright", "credits" or "license()" for more information.
>>> import strings1
This is a single quoted string.
This is a double quoted string.
This is a triple quoted string.
>>>
```

Let's say you have already assigned the values of string 'a' as 'Remember.' and your string 'b' as "Yesterday and Tomorrow.", you have to save the changes you made to strings1, by clicking 'Save'.

119

```
a=('Remember.')
b=("Yesterday and Tomorrow.")
c=("""This is a triple quoted string.""")

print(a)
print(b)
print(c)
```

If you want to combine string 'a' and string 'b', you can go back to your Python shell and import strings1, before combining them.

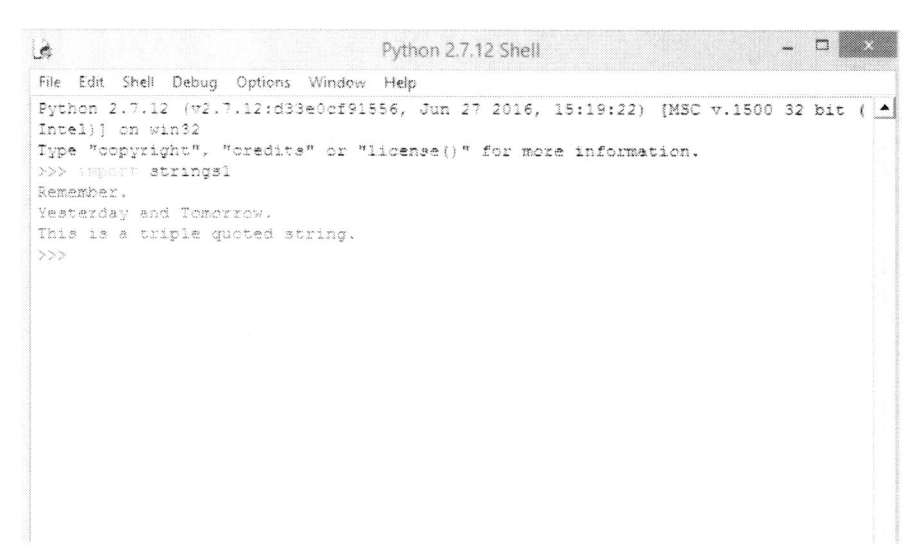

```
Python 2.7.12 (v2.7.12:d33e0cf91556, Jun 27 2016, 15:19:22) [MSC v.1500 32 bit (Intel)] on win32
Type "copyright", "credits" or "license()" for more information.
>>> import strings1
Remember.
Yesterday and Tomorrow.
This is a triple quoted string.
>>>
```

Now, you can combine them, by using the statement or command:

print (a + b),

and then press 'enter'.

```
Python 2.7.12 Shell
File  Edit  Shell  Debug  Options  Window  Help
Python 2.7.12 (v2.7.12:d33e0cf91556, Jun 27 2016, 15:19:22) [MSC v.1500 32 bit (
Intel)] on win32
Type "copyright", "credits" or "license()" for more information.
>>> import strings1
Remember,
Yesterday and Tomorrow.
This is a triple quoted string.
Remember.Yesterday and Tomorrow.
>>>
```

You can do this on your strings1 file itself or in the Python shell. This was done in the file itself, so the combined strings are already displayed when strings1 was imported.

There are other functions that you can take advantage of, such as printing any of the strings repeatedly.

If you want to print string 'b' repeatedly (example: 200 times), you can use the statement: print(b asterisk 200).

print (b * 200)

This will print your 'b' string = "Yesterday and Tomorrow." 200 times. The long method is using the command:

print (b + b + b ... (until it reaches 200), which is a tedious task.

You can enter this function or command in your strings1 file, and then go back to your Python shell and import strings1.

121

See image below.

```
a=('Remember.')
b=("Yesterday and Tomorrow.")
c=("""This is a triple quoted string.""")

print(a)
print(b)
print(c)



print(b * 200)
```

The results will be displayed in your shell, when the file (strings1) is imported. See image below.

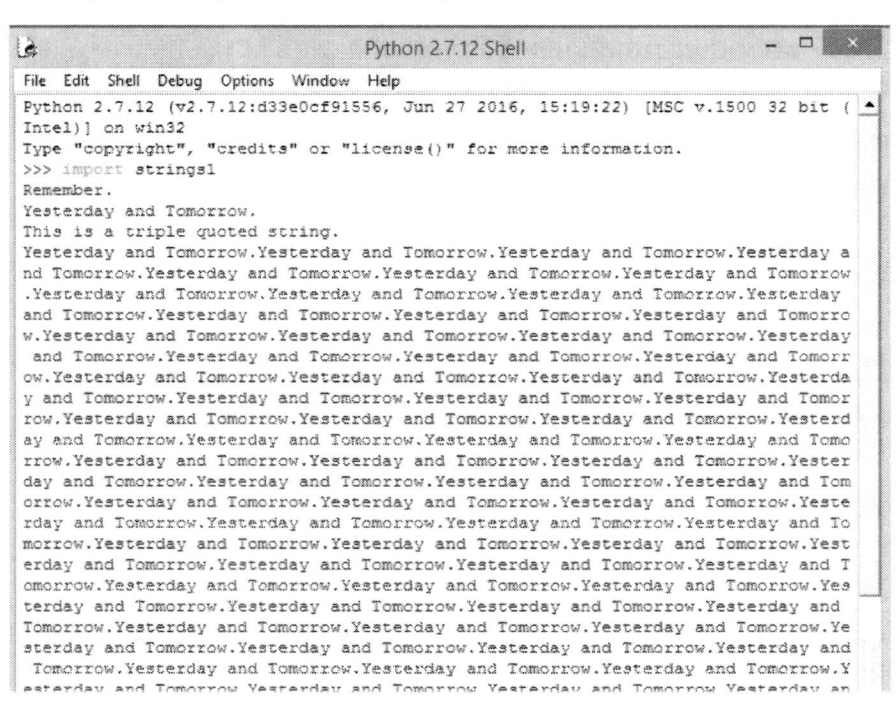

```
Python 2.7.12 (v2.7.12:d33e0cf91556, Jun 27 2016, 15:19:22) [MSC v.1500 32 bit (Intel)] on win32
Type "copyright", "credits" or "license()" for more information.
>>> import strings1
Remember.
Yesterday and Tomorrow.
This is a triple quoted string.
Yesterday and Tomorrow.Yesterday and Tomorrow.Yesterday and Tomorrow.Yesterday and Tomorrow.Yesterday and Tomorrow.Yesterday and Tomorrow.Yesterday and Tomorrow.Yesterday and Tomorrow.Yesterday and Tomorrow.Yesterday and Tomorrow.Yesterday and Tomorrow.Yesterday and Tomorrow.Yesterday and Tomorrow.Yesterday and Tomorrow.Yesterday and Tomorrow.Yesterday and Tomorrow.Yesterday and Tomorrow.Yesterday and Tomorrow.Yesterday and Tomorrow.Yesterday and Tomorrow.Yesterday and Tomorrow.Yesterday and Tomorrow.Yesterday and Tomorrow.Yesterday and Tomorrow.Yesterday and Tomorrow.Yesterday and Tomorrow.Yesterday and Tomorrow.Yesterday and Tomorrow.Yesterday and Tomorrow.Yesterday and Tomorrow.Yesterday and Tomorrow.Yesterday and Tomorrow.Yesterday and Tomorrow.Yesterday and Tomorrow.Yesterday and Tomorrow.Yesterday and Tomorrow.Yesterday and Tomorrow.Yesterday and Tomorrow.Yesterday and Tomorrow.Yesterday and Tomorrow.Yesterday and Tomorrow.Yesterday and Tomorrow.Yesterday and Tomorrow.Y
esterday and Tomorrow.Yesterday and Tomorrow.Yesterday and Tomorrow.Yesterday an
```

You can also click 'Run' in your strings1 file to show the results. See image below:

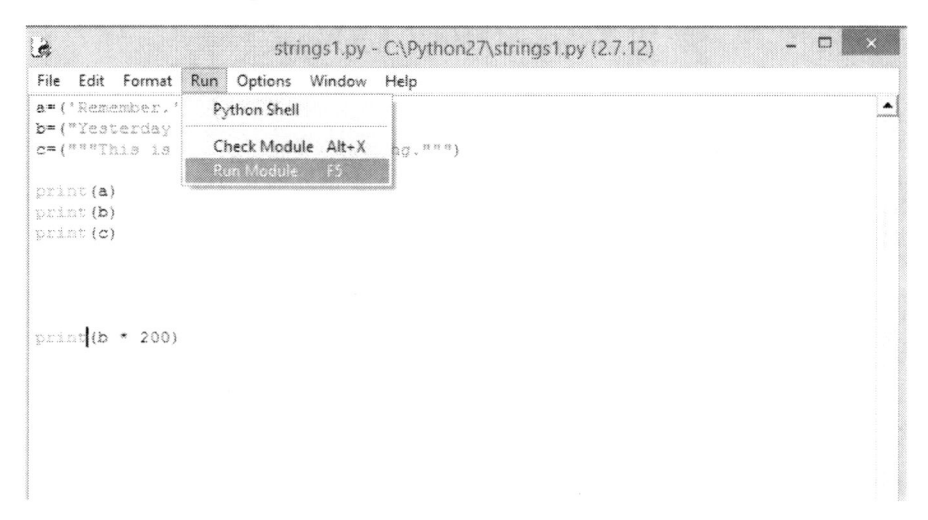

When you click on the 'Run Module' or F5, the same results will appear quickly. See image below:

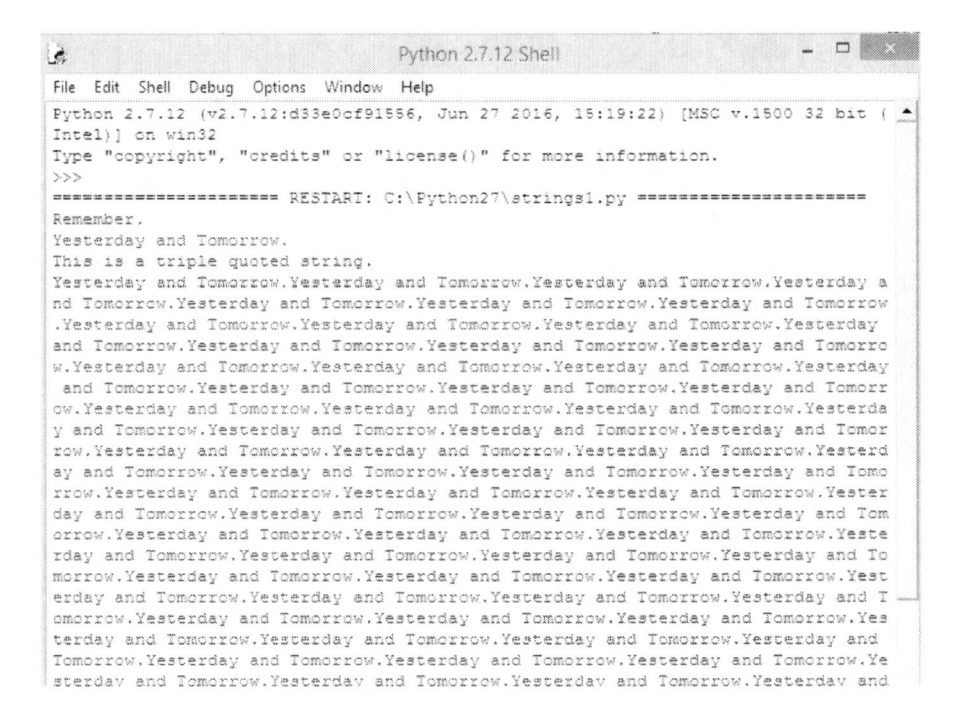

```
Python 2.7.12 Shell
File  Edit  Shell  Debug  Options  Window  Help
Python 2.7.12 (v2.7.12:d33e0cf91556, Jun 27 2016, 15:19:22) [MSC v.1500 32 bit (
Intel)] on win32
Type "copyright", "credits" or "license()" for more information.
>>>
===================== RESTART: C:\Python27\strings1.py ======================
Remember,
Yesterday and Tomorrow.
This is a triple quoted string.
Yesterday and Tomorrow.Yesterday and Tomorrow.Yesterday and Tomorrow.Yesterday a
nd Tomorrow.Yesterday and Tomorrow.Yesterday and Tomorrow.Yesterday and Tomorrow
.Yesterday and Tomorrow.Yesterday and Tomorrow.Yesterday and Tomorrow.Yesterday
and Tomorrow.Yesterday and Tomorrow.Yesterday and Tomorrow.Yesterday and Tomorro
w.Yesterday and Tomorrow.Yesterday and Tomorrow.Yesterday and Tomorrow.Yesterday
 and Tomorrow.Yesterday and Tomorrow.Yesterday and Tomorrow.Yesterday and Tomorr
ow.Yesterday and Tomorrow.Yesterday and Tomorrow.Yesterday and Tomorrow.Yesterda
y and Tomorrow.Yesterday and Tomorrow.Yesterday and Tomorrow.Yesterday and Tomor
row.Yesterday and Tomorrow.Yesterday and Tomorrow.Yesterday and Tomorrow.Yesterd
ay and Tomorrow.Yesterday and Tomorrow.Yesterday and Tomorrow.Yesterday and Tomo
rrow.Yesterday and Tomorrow.Yesterday and Tomorrow.Yesterday and Tomorrow.Yester
day and Tomorrow.Yesterday and Tomorrow.Yesterday and Tomorrow.Yesterday and Tom
orrow.Yesterday and Tomorrow.Yesterday and Tomorrow.Yesterday and Tomorrow.Yeste
rday and Tomorrow.Yesterday and Tomorrow.Yesterday and Tomorrow.Yesterday and To
morrow.Yesterday and Tomorrow.Yesterday and Tomorrow.Yesterday and Tomorrow.Yest
erday and Tomorrow.Yesterday and Tomorrow.Yesterday and Tomorrow.Yesterday and T
omorrow.Yesterday and Tomorrow.Yesterday and Tomorrow.Yesterday and Tomorrow.Yes
terday and Tomorrow.Yesterday and Tomorrow.Yesterday and Tomorrow.Yesterday and
Tomorrow.Yesterday and Tomorrow.Yesterday and Tomorrow.Yesterday and Tomorrow.Ye
sterday and Tomorrow.Yesterday and Tomorrow.Yesterday and Tomorrow.Yesterday and
```

Reminders:

Generally, you cannot combine arguments that are different. For example, integers (numbers) and strings (words).

What you can do is to convert your integer into a word-string by using the prefix, 'str'.

You can create a New File to edit you string1 file with a new string.

In this case, I decided to modify the string1 file. Remember to always save your file, every time you edit or create a new file.

```
strings1.py - C:\Python27\strings1.py (2.7.12)
File  Edit  Format  Run  Options  Window  Help
a=('Remember.')
b=911
```

Take note that integers don't need any parentheses. You cannot add string literals (words) and numbers in one string, so you have to convert the number to a string first, by the key function: str(b).

Next, add 'a' and 'b' with the function/command +:

    print(a + str(b))

Don't forget to enclose your argument in parentheses.

See image below:

Click 'Save', and then click 'Run', and then 'Run Module'.

The combination of arguments 'a' and 'b' will appear, which is:

>   Remember. 911

See image below:

A more specific example is this.

You want to create a personal file about your clients. So, you click on 'File', and then 'New File', just like the previous steps previously discussed.

Let's say you have two arguments, 'Names' and 'Ages', that you would like to combine in your file.

The existing data you have are:

      Names: Potter Richard, Walker Henry, Fell Don, Dean James

      Ages: 20, 34, 41, 32

See image below:

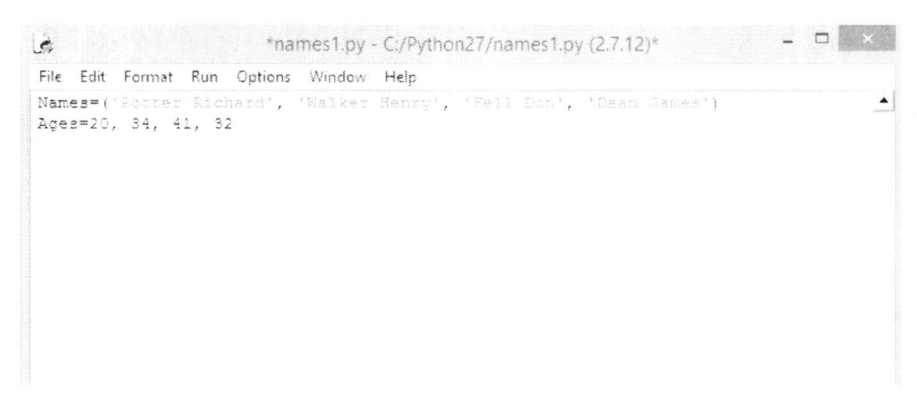

```
Names=('Potter Richard', 'Walker Henry', 'Fell Don', 'Dean James')
Ages=20, 34, 41, 32
```

So, if you want to combine the 'Names' and the 'Ages' strings, your code would be:

      print (Names + Ages)

127

Make sure you save, after entering your code. Enclose each entry with quotes, and separate each entry with a comma. Use parentheses (brackets) for word strings, and no parentheses or quotes for integers (numbers). Don't forget the equal sign when assigning your arguments.

Example:

Names = ("Potter Richard", "Walker Henry", "Fell Don", "Dean James")

Ages = 20, 34, 41, 32

print (Names + Ages)

See image below:

```
Names=('Potter Richard', 'Walker Henry', 'Fell Don', 'Dean James')
Ages=20, 34, 41, 32

print (Names + Ages)
```

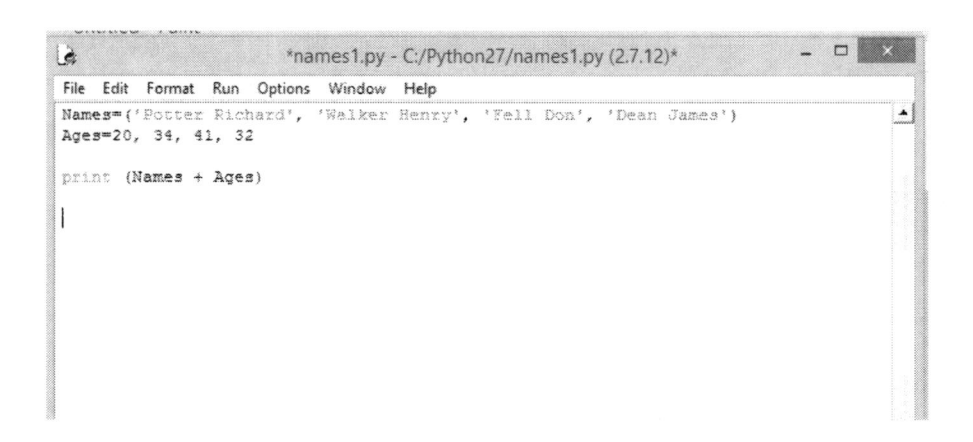

Now, save. Click 'Run', and 'Run Module'. See image below:

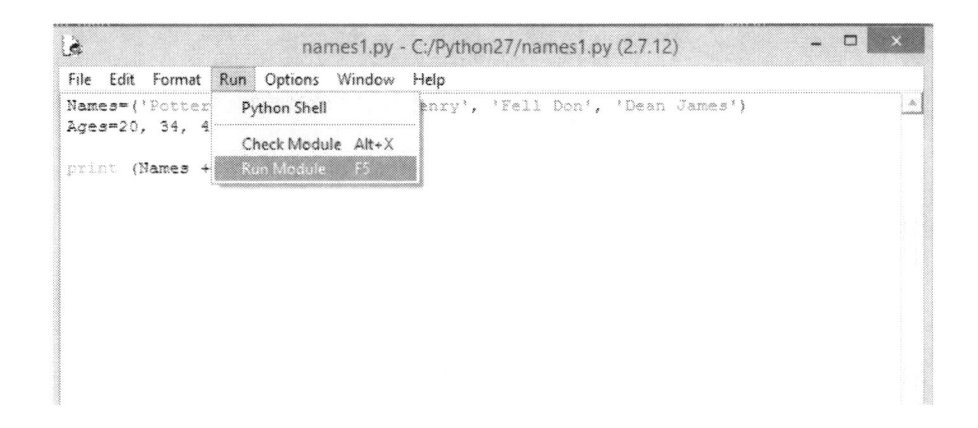

After you had clicked 'Run Module', a new Python shell will appear displaying the results of your code.

See image below:

In this instance, you don't need to create a name string for your integers.

Using the 'join; ( ) key.

You can also use the key, 'join', to combine strings.

Example:

parts=['Richard', 'Potter', 'Probationary']

' '.join(parts)

'Richard Potter Probationary'

' , '.join(parts)

'Richard, Potter, Probationary'

' '.join(parts)

'Richard Potter Probationary'

See image below:

```
>>>
>>> parts=['Richard', 'Potter', 'Probationary']
>>> ' '.join(parts)
'Richard Potter Probationary'
>>> ' , '.join(parts)
'Richard , Potter , Probationary'
>>> ' '.join(parts)
'Richard Potter Probationary'
>>>
```

These are all methods in creating and combining strings.

I hope you can now create your own strings and combine them in your Python shell. The main thing to remember are the key functions (+) and 'join'( ).

Chapter 17: Accessing and Updating Strings

Python strings are one of the most popular method in creating and maintaining codes. They are also very simple to create, as you have read in the previous chapter.

You can access your strings promptly by using the keywords (key) 'import'.

In our examples in the previous chapter, we have saved 'names1' and 'strings1'.

When you need to access them, you can simply import them using your Python shell. Simply type:

    import names1,

And then press 'enter'.

See image below:

```
Python 2.7.12 Shell
File  Edit  Shell  Debug  Options  Window  Help
Python 2.7.12 (v2.7.12:d33e0cf91556, Jun 27 2016, 15:19:22) [MSC v.1500 32 bit (
Intel)] on win32
Type "copyright", "credits" or "license()" for more information.
>>> import names1
('Potter Richard', 'Walker Henry', 'Fell Don', 'Dean James', 20, 34, 41, 32)
```

Of course, you must save your files before you could access them.

For substrings, you can slice through them by using brackets. Please refer to the chapter about slicing lists because the instructions are similar.

131

Anyway, here's one example of accessing your substrings. Let's say your strings are these:

    var1="Welcome to My World."

    var2="Clinical Chemistry"

And you want to get the substrings 1:4 for var1, and the substrings 1:3 for var2. You can enter your statement/code this way: (You can open a 'New File' to do this. Click on 'File', and then 'New File'. Please refer to the chapter on creating files).

Example:

    var1="Welcome to My World."

    var2="Clinical Chemistry"

    print "var1[1:4]: ",var1[1:4]

    print "var2[1:3]: ",var2[1:3]

See image below:

Keep in mind that just like in your indexes, each letter is assigned a number, with the number starting from 0 and then onwards.

Hence, for the first variable [var1], letter W=0; letter e = 1, and so forth. For the second variable [var2], the first letter C is equivalent to 0 and then so forth.

When you press 'Run', and then 'Run Module', on your keypads, a new shell will appear with these results. See image below:

```
Python 2.7.12 Shell
File  Edit  Shell  Debug  Options  Window  Help
Python 2.7.12 (v2.7.12:d33e0cf91556, Jun 27 2016, 15:19:22) [MSC v.1500 32 bit (
Intel)] on win32
Type "copyright", "credits" or "license()" for more information.
>>>
================ RESTART: C:/Python27/Lib/idlelib/edit var1.py ================
var1[1:4]:   elc
var2[1:3]:   li
>>>
```

If you noticed, only the letters that correspond to the numbers are printed - 'elc' from the original word, 'Welcome to My World'.

    W=0,

    e= 1,

    l=2,

    c=3,

    o=4,

    m=5,

    e=6

    and so on

Only letters 'elc' were accessed. As stated in the rule #4 is not included in the results (refer to chapter on slicing lists), when you access indexes or strings.

Likewise, with var2, only 'li' was accessed because of the specified numbers – 1:3; in these examples the colon stands for 'to', and #3 is not included in the results. However, only 1 to 2 letters will appear, so the result printed is 'li', from the original word, 'Clinical Chemistry'.

> C=0,
>
> l=1,
>
> i=2,
>
> n=3,
>
> i=4,
>
> c=5,
>
> a=6,
>
> l=7
>
> and so on

Updating your strings

You can update your strings quickly by indicating what updates you want to do. Let's say you want to add the words "Welcome" from your var1 with "Chemistry" from var2, here's how your code/statement would appear:

Example:

> var1="Welcome to My World."
>
> print "Updated String :- ", var1[:8] + 'Chemistry'

See image below:

```
update1.py - C:/Python27/Lib/idlelib/update1.py (2.7.12)
File  Edit  Format  Run  Options  Window  Help
var1="Welcome to My World."

print "Updated String :- ", var1[ :6] + 'Chemistry'
```

When you click 'Run', and then 'Run Module', a new shell will appear with the results:

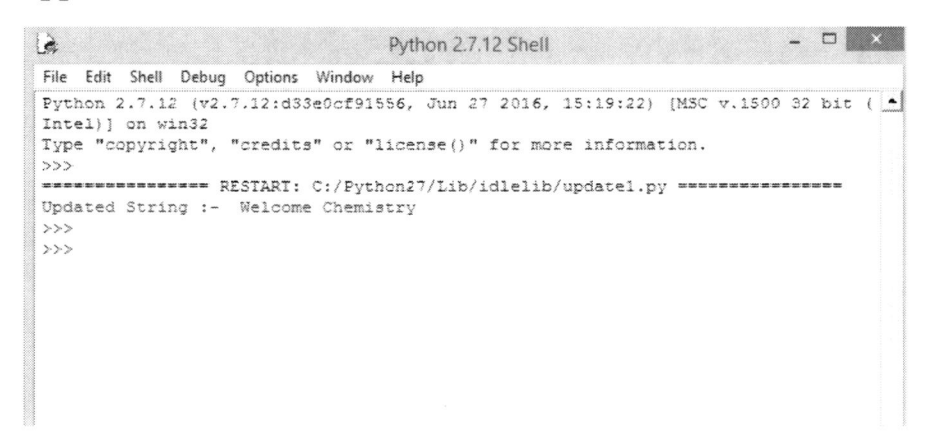

```
Python 2.7.12 Shell
File  Edit  Shell  Debug  Options  Window  Help
Python 2.7.12 (v2.7.12:d33e0cf91556, Jun 27 2016, 15:19:22) [MSC v.1500 32 bit (
Intel)] on win32
Type "copyright", "credits" or "license()" for more information.
>>>
================ RESTART: C:/Python27/Lib/idlelib/update1.py ================
Updated String :- Welcome Chemistry
>>>
>>>
```

It's preferable to open a 'New File' every time you input new data, than typing in the original shell, because some beginners may find the results confusing because of the >>> signs. You can also save the 'New File' easily.

See image below:

135

```
Python 2.7.12 Shell
File  Edit  Shell  Debug  Options  Window  Help
Python 2.7.12 (v2.7.12:d33e0cf91556, Jun 27 2016, 15:19:22) [MSC v.1500 32 bit (
Intel)] on win32
Type "copyright", "credits" or "license()" for more information.
>>>
>>> var1 = "Welcome to my World."
>>>
>>> print "Updated String :- ", var1[ :8] + 'Chemistry'
Updated String :-  Welcome Chemistry
>>>
>>>
```

But if you don't find this confusing, you may opt not to open a 'New File', and type in the new Python shell instead.

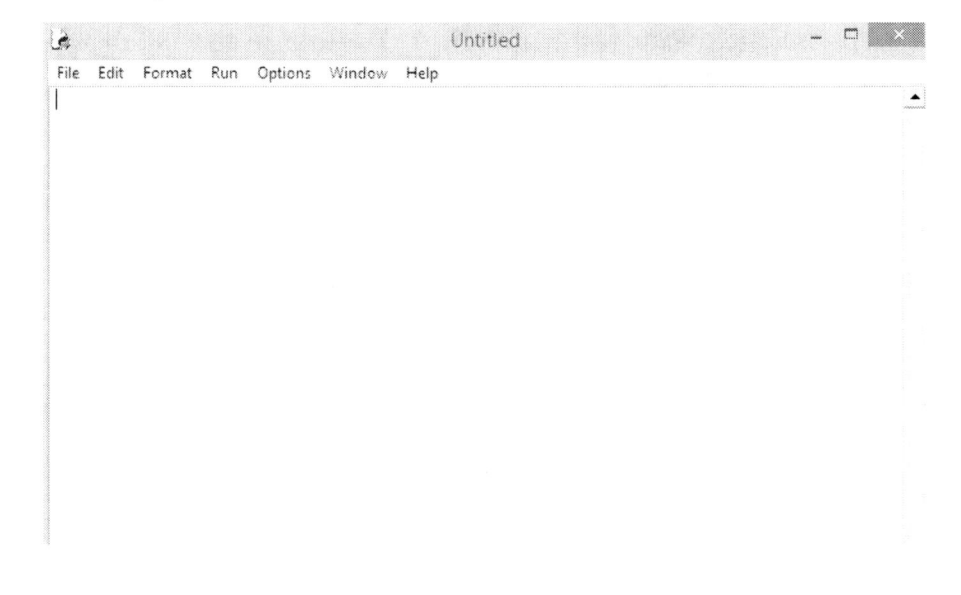

See image below:

```
Untitled
File  Edit  Format  Run  Options  Window  Help
|
```

Chapter 18: Built-in Functions to Format Strings

Python has built-in keys or functions to format your strings. You can access them from your built-in directory.

Here are some of the most common built-in methods:

1. **capitalize ( )**

    This key/function capitalizes the first letter of the string.

    Example:

    > str = "my name is unknown.";

    > print "str.capitalize( ) : ", str.capitalize( )

    See image below:

    ```
    7.py - C:/Python27/Lib/idlelib/7.py (2.7.12)
    File  Edit  Format  Run  Options  Window  Help
    str = "my name is unknown.";
    print "str.capitalize() : ", str.capitalize()
    ```

    When you click 'Run' and 'Run Module', the results will appear in a new shell:

137

```
                          Python 2.7.12 Shell                    -  □  x
File Edit Shell Debug Options Window Help
Python 2.7.12 (v2.7.12:d33e0cf91556, Jun 27 2016, 15:19:22) [MSC v.1500 32 bit (
Intel)] on win32
Type "copyright", "credits" or "license()" for more information.
>>>
=================== RESTART: C:/Python27/Lib/idlelib/7.py ===================
str.capitalize() :  My name is unknown.
>>>
>>>
```

As you can see in the resulting shell, the first letter (m) in the string is already capitalized (M).

2. **count ( ) or count(string, beg=0, end=len(string))**

   Its function is to count the frequency of the occurrence of the specified string, starting from the beginning to the end of the string indexes, or substring indexes.

   Example:

   str = "my name is unknown.";

   sub = "n";

   print "str.count(sub, 3, 10) : ", str.count(sub, 3, 10)

   sub = "unknown";

   print "str.count(sub) : ", str.count(sub)

See image below:

```
str = "my name is unknown.";

sub = "n";
print "str.count(sub, 3, 10) : ", str.count(sub, 3, 10)
sub = "unknown";
print "str.count(sub) : ", str.count(sub)
```

When you click 'Run', and then 'Run Module', the results will appear this way:

```
str.count(sub, 3, 10) :  1
str.count(sub) :  1
```

This means there's only 1 "n" letter counted, and 1 'unknown' word counted in the specified strings.

139

3. center () or center (width, fillchar)

This key/function allows your string to be centered, if indicated, depending on the total of the width columns. The general syntax is this.

Example:

    str.center(width[, fillchar])

    width – indicates the total width of the string.

    fillchar – indicates the filler character.

Example:

    str = "My name is unknown.";

    print "str.center(40, 'a') : ", str.center(40, 'a')

See image below:

```
centerstring.py - C:/Python27/Lib/idlelib/centerstring.py (2.7.12)
File  Edit  Format  Run  Options  Window  Help
str = "My name is unknown.";

print "str.center(40, 'b') : ", str.center(40, 'b')
```

When you click 'Run', and then 'Run Module', a new shell will appear with these results:

```
Python 2.7.12 (v2.7.12:d33e0cf91556, Jun 27 2016, 15:19:22) [MSC v.1500 32 bit (Intel)] on win32
Type "copyright", "credits" or "license()" for more information.
>>>
============== RESTART: C:/Python27/Lib/idlelib/centerstring.py ==============
str.center(40, 'b') :   bbbbbbbbbbMy name is unknown.bbbbbbbbbbb
>>>
>>>
```

4. find ( ), or find (str, beg=0, end=len(str))

This is used to find a string in a string or substring. The second code specifies that the search starts from the beginning and end of the string.

    str – specifies the string to find

    beg – indicates the beginning of the search, which is 0 (start)

    end – indicates the length of the string. If this is not indicated, by default, it would be up to the end of the string.

Example:

    str1 = "My name is unknown.";

    str2 = "name";

141

print str1.find(str2)

print str1.find(str2, 7)

print str1.find(str2, 40)

See image below:

```
str1 = "My name is unknown.";
str2 = "name";

print str1.find(str2)
print str1.find(str2, 7)
print str1.find(str2, 40)
```

After you click 'Run', and then 'Run File', these results will be displayed in a new shell.

```
Python 2.7.12 (v2.7.12:d33e0cf91556, Jun 27 2016, 15:19:22) [MSC v.1500 32 bit (Intel)] on win32
Type "copyright", "credits" or "license()" for more information.
>>>
================ RESTART: C:/Python27/Lib/idlelib/findstring.py ================
3
-1
-1
>>>
>>>
```

The results show -1, meaning the specified string does not exist.

Again, keep in mind the simple string commands, such as:

print stringname[0] = prints the string's first character

print stringname = prints the whole string

print stringname *4 = prints the whole string 4 times.

print stringname + "Great Job! " = prints the whole string + Great Job!

See image below:

```
Python 2.7.12 Shell
File  Edit  Shell  Debug  Options  Window  Help
Python 2.7.12 (v2.7.12:d33e0cf91556, Jun 27 2016, 15:19:22) [MSC v.1500 32 bit (
Intel)] on win32
Type "copyright", "credits" or "license()" for more information.
>>>
>>> mystring2="Tomorrow will be brighter!"
>>>
>>> print mystring2[0]
T
>>>
>>> print mystring2
Tomorrow will be brighter!
>>>
>>> print mystring*4
Traceback (most recent call last):
  File "<pyshell#7>", line 1, in <module>
    print mystring*4
NameError: name 'mystring' is not defined
>>> print mystring2*4
Tomorrow will be brighter!Tomorrow will be brighter!Tomorrow will be brighter!To
morrow will be brighter!
>>>
>>> print mystring2+"Great Job!"
Tomorrow will be brighter!Great Job!
>>>
>>> |
```

Observe from the image above that there was an error in the 3rd code (mystring*4) because the name of the string was wrong. That should have been mystring2.

When the error was corrected in the next print function, the result came out correct – the string was printed 4 times.

The other string commands are discussed in the other chapters.

These are some of the basic string operations that are useful for beginners. As you learn more of Python programming, you will learn about the more complex functions.

When you're ready to proceed to the more advanced methods, you can always access them from the Python program of your saved files.

Chapter 19: Symbols and Operators in Formatting Strings

You can format strings by using the symbols and operators. Chapter 21 has more examples about these operators.

For this particular chapter, the flag operators and integers will be discussed.

Types of integer presentation:

None – indicates a decimal integer and outputs the number in base 10

'b' - stands for **b**inary; it outputs the number in base 2.

'c' - stands for **c**haracter; it converts the integer (number) to a specified Unicode

       character before printing.

'd' - stands for **d**ecimal; it outputs the number in base 10.

'o' - stands for **O**ctal format; it outputs the number in base 8.

'n' - stands for **n**umber; its function is to insert the correct separator characters.

'x' -stands for **Hex** format; for digits above 9, the lowercase letters are used. It

       Outputs the number in base 16.

145

'X'   - this is the same as 'x', the difference only is that the uppercase letters are used,

>for digits above 9.

Common flag characters used for strings:

You can also use conversion flag characters to format your strings. Here are the most common flag characters and their meaning:

'#' – this indicates that the value to be used is the alternate form as defined below.

'-' – this will override the 'o' conversion, if both are given. This indicates that the converted value is adjusted to the left.

'+' – this will override a 'space' flag. This is opposite of the '-' flag.

'0' – this indicates that the values for the numeric values will be zero.

' ' – this blank flag is placed before an empty string or a positive number.

The old operator, %, allows easy formatting of strings. If this operator is still recognized by your Python version, here are some of its functions.

Here are some symbols that you can use with the operator %.

%s – conversion of string using str() before formatting.

%f – real number for floating point

%u- decimal integer (unsigned)

%g – the shorter of %e and %f

%G – the shorter of %E and %f

%e – lowercase 'e' (exponential notation)

%E – uppercase 'E' (exponential notation)

%c – character

%o – octal integer

%i and %d – decimal integers (signed)

%X – uppercase letters (hexadecimal integer)

%x – lowercase letters (hexadecimal integers)

Important Note:

In some new Python versions, curly brackets { } are used and the % is replaced by colons (:).

Example:

'%o4.3f' will be changed with '{:o4.5f}'

There are more complex string commands and codes, but for now, let's focus on these symbols and operators.

See more of the functions and operators through the examples in the other chapters.

Chapter 20: Important Python Semantics

Python has its own syntax and semantics. Before you can write or create your code, you have to be familiar with the Python language.

There are some differences in the Python version 2x and 3x. But generally, it uses some English words instead of punctuations. In this book, most of the discussions are focused on Python 2 because it's more commonly utilized. Python 3 has newer functionalities though, which will be discussed in some of the chapters.

Here are common Python statements and their uses:

1. **'off-side rule'** - where white space indentations, (increased - start or decreased - end), are utilized to indicate whether the block ends or starts.

2. **'pass'** - used as a code block.

3. **'if'** – executes a block of code. It can be used together with 'else'. A combination with 'else', gives the 'else-if' ('elif').

4. **'class'** – commonly used in project-oriented programming, and executing a block of code; the code can be attached to a class.

5. **'yield'** – this can be used as a statement and an operator. It is used to implement coroutines.

6. **'def'** – this statement defines a function or a method.

7. **'for'** – it iterates an object and indicates that the element/s can be utilized by the attached block.

8. **'assert'** – it's used to determine statements that should apply during debugging.

9. **'while'** – executes a block of code, as long as it's true.

10. **'with'** – it encloses a code block, and acquires a lock before the block of code is run.

11. **'try'** – this statement ascertains that the clean-up code black is run, and that exceptions are handled properly.

You can refer to chapter 6 for the type of Python statements.

Chapter 21: Operators and Their Functions

Operators are essential in writing your Python codes. In this chapter we will be discussing about the Logical and Comparison operators.

1. **Logical operators**

    - **and** – (A and B) is FALSE. When you use the 'and' operator. Both conditions (A and B) should be true. If not, the result will display 'False'.

    - **or**   - (A and B) is TRUE. If one condition is true, the result will show
         "True'.

        Some programmers call them the Boolean Operators. They are used to connect sentences, present an option, or an inclusion or exclusion of something.

2. **Comparison operators (use to compare values)**

!=	not equal
==	equal
>	greater than
<	less than
>=	greater than or equal to
<=	less than or equal to

You can use these operators with the 'if' statement, or in any syntax where they can be useful.

Reminder:

The symbol = means you're assigning a value, and == means you're comparing the values.

Example #1:

```
If 3<4:
print ('true')
```

If the statement is true, when you press 'enter' or execute, 'True' will be printed.

See image below:

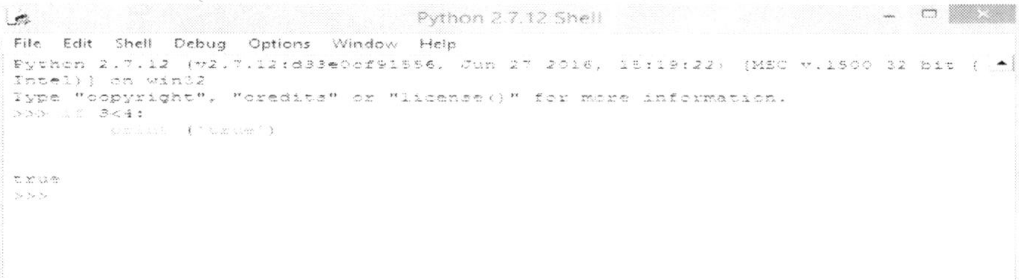

You can also use the operators freely. Always press 'enter' to display results. See image below:

```
Python 2.7.12 (v2.7.12:d33e0cf91556, Jun 27 2016, 15:19:22) [MSC v.1500 32 bit (
Intel)] on win32
Type "copyright", "credits" or "license()" for more information.
>>>
>>> 7!=12
True
>>>
>>> 3>13
False
>>> 5<=7
True
>>>
>>> 13>=12
True
>>>
>>> 15==14
False
>>>
>>> 7<6
False
>>>
>>>
```

You can also use the 'and' operator this way to determine if the statements are 'true' or 'false'.

Example:

   If 7>12 and 12>15:
   If 7>12 or 12>15:

See image below:

```
Python 2.7.12 Shell
File Edit Shell Debug Options Window Help
Python 2.7.12 (v2.7.12:d33e0cf91556, Jun 27 2016, 15:19:22) [MSC v.1500 32 bit (
Intel)] on win32
Type "copyright", "credits" or "license()" for more information.
>>>
>>> 7>12 and 12<15
False
>>>
>>> 7>12 or 12<15
True
>>>
>>>
```

Notice the different results for the 'and' and 'or' operators.

The 'in' operator can determine if the value is present in a string:

Example:

You have this in your string:

  mystring=[1, 2, 3, 4, 5]

And you want to know if 1 is present in the string, simply enter this statement:

  1 in string

And then press 'enter'. The result will display 'True', if 1 is indeed found in the string.

See image below:

153

```
>>>
>>>
>>> string = [1,2,3,4,5]
>>> 1 in string
True
>>>
```

The Python operators can help you create your modules or files. Use them freely and don't be afraid to experiment.

Python is still a developing language; you may be able to discover something new.

Chapter 22: Using 'IF ELSE' Statements

In Python, you can use various condition statements. However, you have to ascertain that you follow the Python syntax rules and indentation. One of these rules is to provide an indentation after the 'if' and 'else' statements, when you enter their codes. Simply press the tab once to provide the indentation.

Anyway, the program will assist you in determining errors in your Python syntax. If there's an error, it will display the errors, and what's wrong with them. You can also press for help, if you're lost in the sea of Python lingo.

Therefore, relax and enjoy the experience.

Functions

The 'IF ELSE' statements, which execute codes, are generally used to compare values, or determine their correctness. 'if' is expressed, if the condition is 'true', while 'else' is expressed when the condition is 'false'.

General code is:

>   if expression:
>   Statement/s
>   else:
>   Statement/s

Example:

Assign a base statement first. Let's say you're teaching chemistry to freshmen college students and you want to encourage them to attend your tutorials. You can compose this Python code:

> hours = float(input('How many hours can you allot for your chemistry tutorials?'))
> if hours < 1:
>   print ('You need more time to study.')
> else:
>   print ('Great! Keep it up!')
> print ('Chemistry needs more of your time.')

From your original Python shell open a New File where you can create your code. Write your code as shown in the image below:

Take not of the indentations and signs. Save the file, and click 'Run', and then "Run Module'.

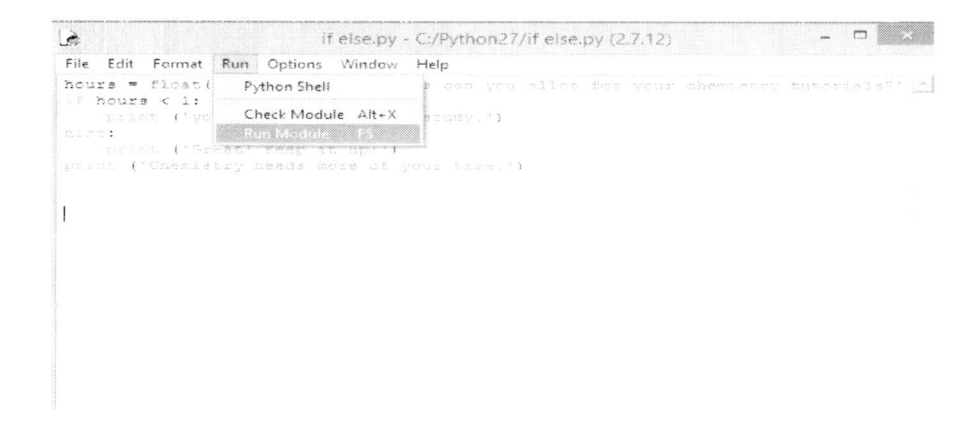

A new shell will appear, where you can test if your code is correct. In this example, this shell (box) will appear:

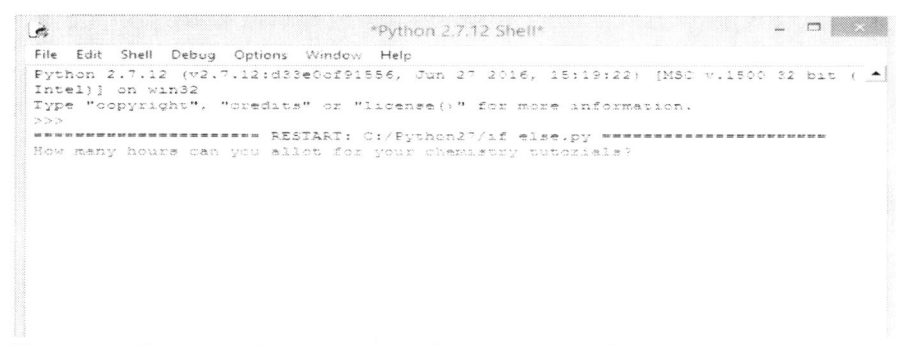

Your student or the user can then answer the question.

Let's say the student has decided to allot 3 hours for his tutorial, thus he typed 3.

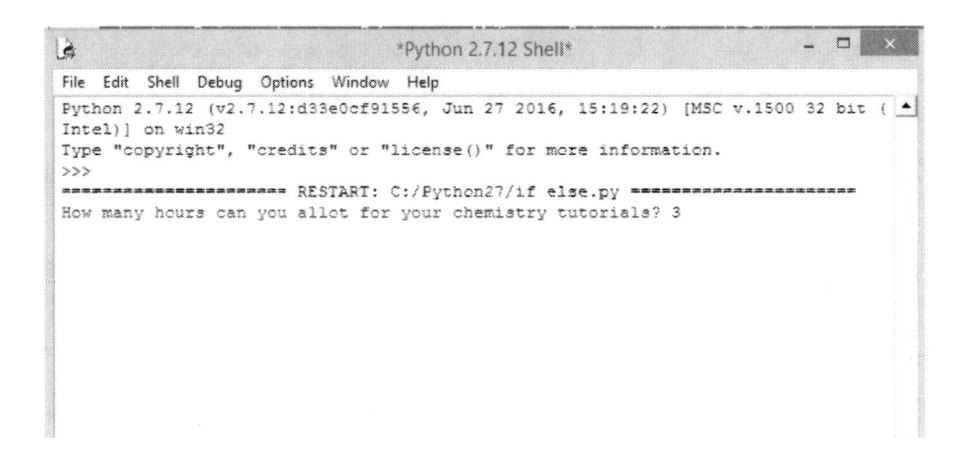

```
*Python 2.7.12 Shell*
File  Edit  Shell  Debug  Options  Window  Help
Python 2.7.12 (v2.7.12:d33e0cf91556, Jun 27 2016, 15:19:22) [MSC v.1500 32 bit (
Intel)] on win32
Type "copyright", "credits" or "license()" for more information.
>>>
==================== RESTART: C:/Python27/if else.py ====================
How many hours can you allot for your chemistry tutorials? 3
```

When the student presses 'enter' or execute, the result will print or display the 'if' and 'else' codes that you have specified.

Since the entered number is more than 1, the 'else' statement is printed or displayed.

See image below:

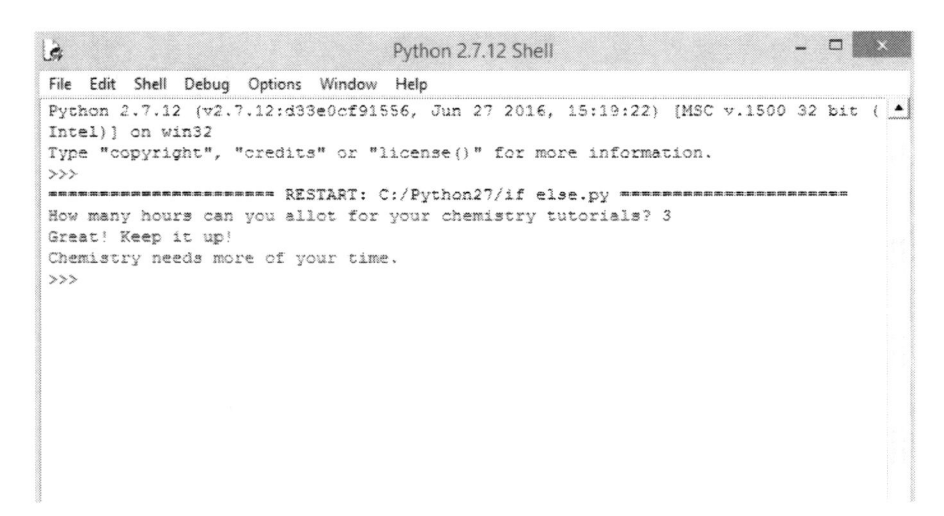

```
Python 2.7.12 Shell
File  Edit  Shell  Debug  Options  Window  Help
Python 2.7.12 (v2.7.12:d33e0cf91556, Jun 27 2016, 15:19:22) [MSC v.1500 32 bit (
Intel)] on win32
Type "copyright", "credits" or "license()" for more information.
>>>
==================== RESTART: C:/Python27/if else.py ====================
How many hours can you allot for your chemistry tutorials? 3
Great! Keep it up!
Chemistry needs more of your time.
>>>
```

Reminders:

1. Always save any 'New File'.

2. Notice that the 'if' and 'else' statements are indented.

3. The 'if' statement is: print('You need more time to study.'), while the
    'else' statement is: print('Great! Keep it up!).

4. The 'if' statement will be printed, if the hours for tutorials inputted by
    the user is less than 1 hour; the 'else' statement will be printed if the hours for tutorials inputted is more than 1 hour.

5. Don't forget the colon (:), after the 'if'' and 'else' conditions.

6. You can have multiple codes/statements in your 'if or 'else' conditions.
    Just remember to indent them.

7. Quotes are also used in the print functions, and parentheses have
    enclosed the sentences to be printed.

In summary, the 'if' and 'else' statements are opposites. Either conditions will be printed based on the condition given.

Chapter 23: Using ELIF Statements

The next type of statement is the 'elif' statement. "elif' is the combination of 'else' and 'if'.

These statements are used when there are more than two choices, and you want to compare various conditions.

The general Python syntax for 'elif' statements is this:

>   if condition1:
>   Statement for condition1
>   elif condition2
>   Statement for condition2
>   elif condition3
>   Statement for condition3
>   elif condition4
>   Statement for condition4
>   elif condition5
>   Statement for condition5
>   else:
>   Statement for false

Example:

You have encoded the grades of your students, and you want to give some encouraging words. You can compose the code below:

>   score=input('Type your grade in my subject.")
>
>   if score >= 75:
>   print ('Passed. You can do better.')
>   elif score >= 80:

```
        print ('Good job.')
    elif score >= 85:
        print ('Great!')
    elif score >= 90:
        print ('Excellent.')
    else:
        print ('Failed. You still have the chance. Study harder')
```

See image below:

```
score=input('Type your grade in my subject.')
if score >= 75:
    print ('Passed. You can do better.')
elif score >= 80:
    print ('Good job.')
elif score >= 85:
    print ('Great!')
elif score >= 90:
    print ('Excellent.')
else:
    print ('Failed. You still have the chance. Study harder')
```

Save and click 'Run', and then 'Run Module'. A new shell will appear. See image below:

Your student can then enter his grade. If the grade of your student is 80, the result will print the statement you have specified in your code.

```
Python 2.7.12 Shell
File Edit Shell Debug Options Window Help
Python 2.7.12 (v2.7.12:d33e0cf91556, Jun 27 2016, 15:19:22) [MSC v.1500 32 bit (
Intel)] on win32
Type "copyright", "credits" or "license()" for more information.
>>>
================== RESTART: C:/Python27/Lib/idlelib/4.py ==================
Type your grade in my subject.80
Passed. You can do better.
>>>
```

If you have a keen eye, you will notice that there's something wrong with the code, because all the other values fall within the range of the first 'if' statement.

You can remedy this by editing your syntax:

> Grades = input('Type your grade in my subject.')
>
> if Grades >=75:
>   print ('Passed. You can do better.')
> if grades <75:
>   print ('Failed. Keep studying.')
> else:
>   print ('Not enrolled.')

See image below:

```
grades2.py - C:/Python27/grades2.py (2.7.12)
File  Edit  Format  Run  Options  Window  Help
Grades = input('Type your grade in my subject.')
if Grades >=75:
    print ('Passed. You can do better.')
if grades <75:
    print ('Failed. Keep studying.')
else:
    print ('Not enrolled.')
```

If the student typed 75, the statement specified in your 'if' condition will appear.

See image below:

```
                    Python 2.7.12 Shell
File  Edit  Shell  Debug  Options  Window  Help
Python 2.7.12 (v2.7.12:d33e0cf91556, Jun 27 2016, 15:19:22) [MSC v.1500 32 bit (
Intel)] on win32
Type "copyright", "credits" or "license()" for more information.
>>>
==================== RESTART: C:/Python27/grades2.py ====================
Type your grade in my subject.
==================== RESTART: C:/Python27/grades2.py ====================
Type your grade in my subject.75
Passed. You can do better.
```

You can edit your Python code until you obtain the desired results. You can also turn it into a loop by adding 'while'. Refer to the chapter on loops.

163

Chapter 24: Functions of Python Loops

There are two types of Python loops; the 'while' and the 'for'. This word would be most probably new to you. But bear in mind that everything can be learned, and you will benefit tremendously with your basic knowledge of Python. So, cheer up and keep going.

What is a loop?

As defined in the previous chapter, it is a symbol used to represent repeated (iterated) word/s or sentence/s in Python programming. Anything that is being repeatedly used can employ a loop (a piece of code). Hence, it facilitates the task that you would want to accomplish.

Types of loops

1. **The 'while' loop** – this is used to implement a piece of code repeatedly.

   Example:

   Let's say you have these values: a – for individual numbers; t – for sum of the numbers:

   a=1

   t=0

And you want the user to 'Enter numbers to add to the total.', you write the code for the 'while; loop this way:

   print ('Enter numbers to add to the total.')

   print ('Enter x to quit.')

(Now use the 'while' function to allow the action to become repetitive.)

```
while a ! = 0:
        print ('Current Total:  ', t)
        a = float(input("Number? '))
        a = float (a)
        t+ = a
print ('Grand Total = ', t)
```
This is how your code will look like.

Example:

```
a=1
t=0
print ('Enter numbers to add to the total.')
print ('Enter x to quit.')
while a ! = 0:
        print ('Current Total:  ', t)
        a = float(input("Number? '))
        a = float (a)
        t+ = a
print ('Grand Total = ', t)
```

See image below:

```
a=1
t=0
print ('Enter numbers to add to the total.')
print ('Enter x to quit.')
while a!=0:
    print ('Current Total:  ', t)
    a = float(input('Number? '))
    a = float(a)
    t += a
print ('Grand Total = ', t)
```

Then, click 'Run', and then 'Run Module'. The box below will appear:

```
>>>
==================== RESTART: C:/Python27/Lib/idlelib/1.py ==========
=========
Enter numbers to add to the total.
Enter x to quit.
('Current Total:  ', 0)
Number?
==================== RESTART: C:/Python27/Lib/idlelib/1.py ==========
=========
Enter numbers to add to the total.
Enter x to quit.
('Current Total:  ', 0)
Number?
```

This code will allow the user to enter his number and the program will compute for the total.

The user can also subtract numbers, and the program will still get the total.

Let's say the user has entered the following numbers: 1289, 6709 and 45678, the results will appear this way:

```
==================== RESTART: C:/Python27/Lib/idlelib/1.py ==========
=========
Enter numbers to add to the total.
Enter x to quit.
('Current Total:   ', 0)
Number? 1289
('Current Total:   ', 1289.0)
Number? 6709
('Current Total:   ', 7998.0)
Number? 45678
('Current Total:   ', 53676.0)
Number?
                                                           Ln: 82  Col: 8
```

The program or code continues, and a user can add (enter) as many numbers as he wants.

The loop will continue obtaining the sum of the entered numbers, repeatedly, until you press 'x' to 'exit'.

You or any user can also subtract numbers (examples – 90, and then -3456) and the loop will display the total.

See image below:

167

```
==================== RESTART: C:/Python27/Lib/idlelib/1.py ==========
=========
Enter numbers to add to the total.
Enter x to quit.
('Current Total:   ', 0)
Number? 1289
('Current Total:   ', 1289.0)
Number? 6709
('Current Total:   ', 7998.0)
Number? 45678
('Current Total:   ', 53676.0)
Number? 879
('Current Total:   ', 54555.0)
Number? -90
('Current Total:   ', 54465.0)
Number? -3456
('Current Total:   ', 51009.0)
Number?
                                                        Ln: 88  Col: 8
```

The code is useful, as long as 'x' is not entered. Once 'x' is entered, the loop will end and the program won't be useful anymore - unless you save it.

In these examples, you have to apply the basic rules in Python syntax, or statement.

Look out for the double parentheses. Use the function 'print', whenever you want your reader, or user to read the text, and don't forget to enclose your variables or elements in quotes.

2. **The second type is the 'for' loop.**

The 'for' loop can be used in printing elements, one by one. An example is this:

b= (9, 4, 2, 8, 12, 5, 67)

If, you want to print the numbers above, one by one, you can use the 'for' loop, this way:

for num in b:

(num – holds the values of each element in b.)

Hence, your final code would be:

> for num in b:
>> print (num)

See image below:

```
                        Python 2.7.12 Shell                    _ □ ×
File  Edit  Shell  Debug  Options  Window  Help
Python 2.7.12 (v2.7.12:d33e0cf91556, Jun 27 2016, 15:19:22) [MSC v.1500 32 bit (
Intel)] on win32
Type "copyright", "credits" or "license()" for more information.
>>> b=(9, 4, 2, 8, 12, 5, 67)
>>> for num in b:
        print (num)

9
4
2
8
12
5
67
>>>
```

For the 'while' loop, the condition must be true to be able to operate; unlike for the 'for' loop; it works even if the condition is not true.

169

Chapter 25: Creating and Using Tuples

Tuples as defined earlier, are similar to strings. Tuples and strings are the same - you cannot modify them because they are immutable (unchangeable).

This is because once you have assigned the values, they can no longer be changed. There are methods to the create new Tuples and strings though, as mentioned below.

Differences of Tuples and Lists

Lists use square brackets [ ], while Tuples use parentheses ( ). Heterogeneous data is also possible with Tuples. On the other hand, lists usually have homogenous data.

Uses of Tuples

1. When the data are converted to tuples, it can return values in groups. Generally, without Tuple, 'returns' provide only a single value.
2. They can be used as dictionary keys because they are immutable.
3. They are protected from accidental modifications.
4. Iteration is quicker with Tuples because of their nature.
5. They allow the grouping of related data that may be different in data types.

Built-in functions

There are built-in functions for Tuple that you must know. These are:

1. **tuple(seq)** – this is an important function because it can convert your lists to Tuples.

   Example: If you want to convert your list1 to tuple

   list1 = ('Vivian Dixon', 'single', 25)

   tuple(list1)

   See image below:

   ```
   >>>
   >>> tuple(list1)
   ('Vivian Dixon', 'single', 25)
   >>>
   >>>
   ```

   When you print it, the results will be:

   ```
   >>>
   >>> print tuple(list1)
   ('Vivian Dixon', 'single', 25)
   >>>
   >>>
   ```

2. **cmp(tuple1, tuple2)** – this function can compare two Tuples.

   Example:

171

tuple1- ('cde',325)

tuple2 – ('fgh', 525)

cmp(tuple1, tuple2)

3. **min(tuple)** – it shows the minimum values found in your Tuples.

   Example:

   tuple=(3,6,9,11,13,15,20)

   min(tuple)

   print min(tuple)

See image below:

```
>>>
>>> tuple=(3,6,9,11,13,15,20)
>>>min(tuple)
>>> print min(tuple)
3
>>>
>>>
```

4. **max(tuple)** – it shows the maximum values found in your Tuples.

Example:

tuple =(1256, 1259, 1224, 1231, 1214)

max(tuple)

print max(tuple)

You can also press 'enter', after max(tuple), and the maximum value will appear, which is 1259.

See image below:

```
>>>
>>>
>>> tuple =(1256, 1259, 1224, 1231, 1214)
>>> max(tuple)
1259
>>>
>>>
```

If you have decided to open a 'New File', you can access the results, by clicking 'Run' and then. 'Run Module'.

See image below:

After you have clicked 'Run', and 'Run Module', the result will appear in a new shell:

See image below:

The same result will appear, which is 1259.

5. **len(tuple)** – it specifies the total lengths of your Tuples.

Example:

tuple =(1256, 1259, 1224, 1231, 1214)

len(tuple)

print len(tuple)

See image below:

```
tuple =(1256, 1259, 1224, 1231, 1214)
len(tuple)

print len(tuple)
```

When you click 'Run', and 'Run Module', the results will appear in a new shell, which is 5.

```
==================== RESTART: C:/Python27/Lib/idlelib/12.py ===============
5
>>>
>>>
>>>
```

If you decide to use the original shell, without creating a 'New File', be sure to observe the correct indentation because your statement or code might not be able to work.

175

```
>>> tuple =(1256, 1259, 1224, 1231, 1214)
>>> len(tuple)
>>>
>>> print len(tuple)
5
>>>
>>>
```

You will be obtaining the same results, whatever method you decide to use.

But for beginners, creating a 'New File' is advisable because you can edit your code all you want, before running it.

Changing Tuples

Tuples are immutable; however, Tuples can be sliced using a bracket [ ] and a colon (:), and concatenated or combined using the + sign. If the data type is mutable, the nested elements can also be changed.

The elements in a Tuple can be repeated, as many times as you want, with the operator (*) asterisk.

Creating Tuples

Step #1 – Place all elements inside the parentheses ( )

All the items that you would want to convert to a Tuple must be separated by commas, and enclosed by parentheses.

When the number-element is only one, the ending comma must still be added, to indicate that the data is a tuple.

Examples:

tup1 = ( )

tup2 = ("Jean", "Walker", 2004, "female", "fourth year");

tup3 = ("October", 20, 2014, "Saturday");

tup4 = (1, 2, 3, 4, 5, 6, 7, 8, 9, 10);

Notice that the first Tuple is empty, and tup3 has integers, and word elements inside the parentheses.

The words are enclosed in quotes'; separated by commas, and all items are enclosed inside parentheses. It can also contain lists, floats and other items.

Some programmers don't use the parentheses to enclose the items in a Tuple. Choose what's more convenient for you.

When elements are not enclosed in a parentheses (Tuples) or square brackets (strings), they are automatically identified as Tuples.

Step #2 – Access the values of your Tuples

You can assess the values of your Tuples by printing them. Based on the values of your Tuples above, you can choose what to print.

Keep in mind that your indexes in Tuples is the same as your lists – they start at 0.

Example:

177

print "tup2[2]: ", tup2[2]

print "tup3[1:3]: ", tup3[1:3]

See image below:

```
tup1 = ( )
tup2 = ('Jean', 'Walker', 2004, 'female', 'fourth year');
tup3 = ('October', 20, 2014, 'Saturday');
tup4 = (1, 2, 3, 4, 5, 6, 7, 8, 9, 10);

print "tup2[2]: ", tup2[2]
print "tup3[1:3]: ", tup3[1:3]
```

A 'New File' was created for these statements, so click 'Run' and then 'Run Module'.

The results will appear in a new shell.

See image below:

```
Python 2.7.12 Shell
File Edit Shell Debug Options Window Help
Python 2.7.12 (v2.7.12:d33e0cf91556, Jun 27 2016, 15:19:22) [MSC v.1500 32 bit (
Intel)] on win32
Type "copyright", "credits" or "license()" for more information.
>>>
================== RESTART: C:/Python27/Lib/idlelib/tup1.py ==================
tup2[2]:  2004
tup3[1:3]:   (20, 2014)
>>>
```

Keep in mind that the 1:3 indicates that the items printed will start at 1 up to 2, and not 3.

In the example above, the items are numbered this way:

tup2 = (#0 -"Jean", #1-"Walker", #2- 2004, #3 -"female", #4 - "fourth year");

Thus, #2 in tup2 = 2004 (which was printed)

tup3 = (#0 - "October", #1 - 20, #2 - 2014, #3 - "Saturday");

Thus, tup3[1:3] = 20, 2014 (which was printed)

This is because #1 is 20 and #2 is 2014; (1:3 is actually 1 to 2 only, and not 1 to 3). If you want to print 'Saturday', you have to change it to [1:4]

Deleting Tuples

As mentioned repeatedly, you cannot delete a Tuple file, but you can create a new one, and omit the elements you don't

179

want to include. You can then delete the whole Tuple by using the key 'del'.

Example:

tup2 = ("Jean", "Walker", 2004, "female", "fourth year");

print tup2

See image below:

```
>>> tup2 = ('Jean', 'Walker', 2004, 'female', 'fourth year');
>>> print tup2
('Jean', 'Walker', 2004, 'female', 'fourth year')
>>>
```

Then add the statement for deletion:

del tup2;

print "after deleting tup2 : "

print tup2

When you enter, print tup2, the result below will appear:

```
>>>
>>> print tup2
Traceback (most recent call last):
  File "<pyshell#16>", line 1, in <module>
    print tup2
NameError: name 'tup2' is not defined
>>> |
```

Your tup2 file is no longer accessible because it has been deleted.

Updating Tuples

As previously mentioned, the elements in Tuples cannot be changed. Nonetheless, you can update your Tuples by getting items from your old Tuples to create a new Tuple.

Example:

>   tup5 = tup2 + tup3
>
>   print tup5

See image below:

```
>>>
>>> tup5=tup2 + tup3
>>> print tup5
('Jean', 'Walker', 2004, 'female', 'fourth year', 'October', 20, 2014, 'Saturday')
>>>
>>>
```

When you press 'enter', the result is a new Tuple (tup5), composed of the elements of tup2 and tup3.

181

Now, let's proceed to the basic operations for Tuple. What are these operations that you need as you start to learn Python? Here they are:

Basic Operations

The basic operations for Tuple are the same with strings.

1. **Repetition** – use the key (*), asterisk.

    Example:

    tup2 = ("Jean", "Walker", 2004, "female", "fourth year");

    tup2*2

    When you press 'enter', the result would be:

    ```
    >>>
    >>>
    >>> tup2 = ("Jean", "Walker", 2004, "female", "fourth year");
    >>> tup2*2
    ('Jean', 'Walker', 2004, 'female', 'fourth year', 'Jean', 'Walker', 2004, 'female', 'fourth year')
    >>>
    ```

    The elements of tup2 have been printed twice, as specified by your statement (tup2*2).

2. **Concatenation** – use the key (+) plus sign.

    Example:

tup2 = ("Jean", "Walker", 2004, "female", "fourth year");

tup3 = ("Clinical Chemistry", 80,);

print tup2 + tup3

See image below:

A 'New File' was opened, therefore, the 'Run' and 'Run Module' menu were clicked. The result that came up in a new shell was the combination of the elements of tup2 and tup3.

3. **Iteration** – it works the same way as strings.
4. **Length** – it works the same way as strings, using the key, 'len'.

```
>>>
>>> len((1, 2, 3))
3
>>>
>>>
```

You can always refer to the strings chapter anytime you want to.

Chapter 26: How to Convert Python Data

In Python programming, data can be converted from one type to another. Here are simple steps of doing this.

For converting an integer to a character, use the key 'chr', like this:

Example:

    chr(x)

Where 'chr' stands for character, and x stands for the integers (numbers).

Let's say you want to convert the integers: 13, 4, 10, 7 and 14. Simply type the key 'chr' and substitute the numbers for the x value.

Example:

    chr(13)
    chr(4)
    chr(10)
    chr(7)
    chr(14)

When you press 'enter' the numbers are converted into characters. See image below:

```
Python 2.7.12 Shell
File Edit Shell Debug Options Window Help
Python 2.7.12 (v2.7.12:d33e0cf91556, Jun 27 2016, 15:19:22) [MSC v.1500 32 bit (
Intel)] on win32
Type "copyright", "credits" or "license()" for more information.
>>> chr(13)
'\r'
>>> chr(4)
'\x04'
>>> chr(10)
'\n'
>>> chr(7)
'\x07'
>>> chr(14)
'\x0e'
```

For converting to a string representation, use the key – 'str'.

Examples:

    str(14)
    str(23)
    str(29)

The result will be:

```
>>>
>>>
>>> str(14)
'14'
>>> str(23)
'23'
>>> str(29)
'29'
>>>
```

For converting data to a tuple, use the key 'tuple'. If you want to convert data 'y' and 'x' to tuples, here are the codes:

Examples:

    tuple(string1)
    tuple(names1)

The statement above will convert the files string1 and names1 to Tuple files.

See image below:

```
>>>
>>> tuple('string1')
('s', 't', 'r', 'i', 'n', 'g', '1')
>>>
>>>
>>> tuple('names1')
('n', 'a', 'm', 'e', 's', '1')
>>>
>>>
```

For converting data to a list, use the key, 'list'. For example, you want to convert the data, 'names1' to a list, this code/statement applies:

Example:

    List('names1')

The file names1 is converted into a list file. See image below:

```
Python 2.7.12 Shell
File Edit Shell Debug Options Window Help
Python 2.7.12 (v2.7.12:d33e0cf91556, Jun 27 2016, 15:19:22) [MSC v.1500 32 bit (
Intel)] on win32
Type "copyright", "credits" or "license()" for more information.
>>>
>>> list('names1')
['n', 'a', 'm', 'e', 's', '1']
>>>
>>>
```

187

For converting data to a frozen set, use the key, 'frozenset'. If your data is 'names1' and you want to convert it to a frozen set, see the example below.

Example:

>   frozenset('names1')

When you press 'enter', names1 will be converted to a frozenset. See image below:

```
>>>
>>>
>>> frozenset('names1')
frozenset(['a', 'e', 'm', 'n', '1', 's'])
>>>
>>>
```

For converting data to a set, use the key 'set'. An example is when you want to convert your data, 'names1', to a set, your statement would be:

Example:

>   set('names1')

The result would be:

```
Python 2.7.12 Shell
File  Edit  Shell  Debug  Options  Window  Help
Python 2.7.12 (v2.7.12:d33e0cf91556, Jun 27 2016, 15:19:22) [MSC v.1500 32 bit (
Intel)] on win32
Type "copyright", "credits" or "license()" for more information.
>>>
>>> set('names1')
set(['a', 'e', 'm', 'n', '1', 's'])
>>>
>>>
```

For converting data to an expression string, use the key 'repr'.

Example:

If you want to convert your 'names1' file into an expression string, here's your code:

Example:

>   repr('names1')

After you press 'enter', the result will be this:

```
>>>
>>> repr('names1')
"'names1'"
>>>
>>>
```

For converting your data (integer) to a Unicode character, you can use the key 'unichr'.

Example:

>   unichr(23)

When you press 'enter', the result will be:

```
>>>
>>> unichr(23)
u'\x17'
>>>
>>>
```

For converting one character to its integer value, you can use the key – 'ord'.

Example:

Convert your data ('a') to its integer value. Use this statement:

>	ord('a')
>	ord('b')
>	ord('c')

When you press 'enter', these will be the results:

```
>>>
>>>
>>> ord('a')
97
>>>
>>> ord('b')
98
>>>
>>> ord('c')
99
>>>
```

For converting string data to an integer, use the key 'int'. If you want to convert a string, with a base, to an integer, use this code instead:

>	int(s[,base]).

Substitute your data for s.

Here are other conversions that may prove useful to you:

1. **eval(str)** – this returns an object, after evaluating your specified string.

2. **dict( )** - this creates a dictionary, the value inside the parentheses must be in sequence.
3. **float ( )** – converts the integer or the value inside the parentheses to a floating-point number.
4. **oct( )** – converts the integer or number inside the parentheses to an octal string.

For more complex conversion keywords, you can learn them later on when you have become familiar with these common conversion keys. You can refer too to the other chapters in this book.

Chapter 27: How to Build Your Python Lists

In Python, lists can contain different types of data, such as string values, integers, and other various forms. They can also be iterated (repeated) several times. They can work as arrays, as well.

You can create any list you want and add or remove values from your list. Here's how:

Step #1 – Create your list

You can start creating your lists by using these codes:

>   mylist = [ ]

You're using blank brackets to indicate that there's still no value to your list. You can assign any value; in this example, we will be adding names to the list.

Example:

>   mylist = ['Wilson', 'White', 'Bronson']

When you have typed mylist, and have pressed 'enter', or execute, the contents of your 'mylist' will be displayed. See image below:

```
Python 2.7.12 Shell
File Edit Shell Debug Options Window Help
Python 2.7.12 (v2.7.12:d33e0cf91556, Jun 27 2016, 15:19:22) [MSC v.1500 32 bit (
Intel)] on win32
Type "copyright", "credits" or "license()" for more information.
>>> mylist = []
>>> mylist = ['Wilson', 'White', 'Bronson']
>>> mylist
['Wilson', 'White', 'Bronson']
>>>
```

Remember to enclose your variables with quotes and then brackets.

Take note that the index for the first item is 0, the next item is 1, the next item is 3, and so forth.

In the above example, the index for 'Wilson' is 0; 'White' is 1, and 'Bronson' is 3.

So, if you want to access 'Wilson', you can enter:

Examples:

>   mylist [0]

For 'White':
>   mylist [1]

and for 'Bronson':
>   mylist [2]

See image below:

193

```
Python 2.7.12 Shell
File Edit Shell Debug Options Window Help
Python 2.7.12 (v2.7.12:d33e0cf91556, Jun 27 2016, 15:19:22) [MSC v.1500 32 bit (
Intel)] on win32
Type "copyright", "credits" or "license()" for more information.
>>> mylist = []
>>> mylist
[]
>>> mylist=['Wilson', 'White', 'Bronson']
>>> mylist
['Wilson', 'White', 'Bronson']
>>> mylist[0]
'Wilson'
>>> mylist[1]
'White'
>>> mylist[2]
'Bronson'
>>>
```

You can also do it the reverse way, by using the (-) sign.

Examples:

To access 'Wilson', type:

> mylist [-3] and press enter.

To access 'White, type:

> mylist [-2] and type enter.

To access 'Bronson', type:

> mylist [-1]

Step #2 – Add to your list

You can also add to your list by using the 'append' function.

Example:

      mylist.append ('Cruise')

When you press enter, the item will be added to your list.

Another example is when you want to add the name 'Park' to your list, use the same function:

Example:

      mylist.append('Park')

In the image below, there was an error with the first execution because brackets were used.

It's important to note that when an error occurs in your code or syntax, the results will appear in red.

When the error was corrected by enclosing 'Park' with parentheses, the result was given correctly.
See image below:

```
>>> mylist.append('Cruise')
>>> mylist
['Wilson', 'White', 'Bronson', 'Cruise']
>>> mylist.append['Park']

Traceback (most recent call last):
  File "<pyshell#9>", line 1, in <module>
    mylist.append['Park']
TypeError: 'builtin_function_or_method' object has no attribute '__getitem__'
>>> mylist.append('Park')
>>> mylist
['Wilson', 'White', 'Bronson', 'Cruise', 'Park']
>>>
```

Step #3 – Delete or remove an item from your list

You can do this by using the function keyword 'remove'.

Example: If you want to remove 'Bronson', you use the statement below.

> mylist.remove ('Bronson')

You can continue removing from your list ('Wilson'), using the same function word.
> mylist.remove('Wilson')

This statement will remove 'Bronson' and 'Wilson' from your list.

See image below:

```
>>>
>>>
>>> mylist.remove('Bronson')
>>> mylist
['Wilson', 'White', 'Cruise', 'Park']
>>>
>>> mylist.remove ('Wilson')
>>> mylist
['White', 'Cruise', 'Park']
>>> 
```

Remember to add a dot (.) between the name of your list and the function word.

There are other built-in function words (extend, max, len, print), you can use to edit or change your list. You can also print more than one list simultaneously.

Example:

>   print ('mylist1, mylist2, mylist3)

Chapter 28: Slicing from a List

You can 'slice' your list, to create a new list. Slicing is taking a portion, or selecting (slicing) a part of your list to display.

Keep in mind that the index of your list starts with '0' (zero).

Example #1:

If you want to slice your list of names, you can use a colon (:) to do this. Let's say the name of your list is 'mylist2', and the values you assigned are: a, b, c, d, e, f, g, h, i.

Your syntax would appear this way:

> mylist2 = ['a', 'b', 'c', 'd', 'e', 'f', 'g', 'h', 'i']

See image below:

```
*Python 2.7.12 Shell*
File  Edit  Shell  Debug  Options  Window  Help
Python 2.7.12 (v2.7.12:d33e0cf91556, Jun 27 2016, 15:19:22) [MSC v.1500 32 bit (
Intel)] on win32
Type "copyright", "credits" or "license()" for more information.
>>> mylist2=['a', 'b', 'c', 'd', 'e', 'f', 'g', 'h', 'i']
```

Call (Recall) the data by typing 'mylist2', and then press enter. Your list will appear.

See image below:

```
Python 2.7.12 (v2.7.12:d33e0cf91556, Jun 27 2016, 15:19:22) [MSC v.1500 32 bit (
Intel)] on win32
Type "copyright", "credits" or "license()" for more information.
>>> mylist2=['a', 'b', 'c', 'd', 'e', 'f', 'g', 'h', 'i']
>>>
>>> mylist2
['a', 'b', 'c', 'd', 'e', 'f', 'g', 'h', 'i']
>>>
```

You can slice this list by using the colon sign.

If you want to print from values 'b' to 'e', you can type:

>mylist2 [1:5]

This is because, as previously explained, your indexes start from 0 onwards. Thus, 'a' is zero (0), 'b' = 1, 'c' = 2, and so forth.

When you press 'enter' or execute, the values, 'b' to 'e', will appear.

See image below:

199

```
Python 2.7.12 (v2.7.12:d33e0cf91556, Jun 27 2016, 15:19:22) [MSC v.1500 32 bit (
Intel)] on win32
Type "copyright", "credits" or "license()" for more information.
>>> mylist2=['a', 'b', 'c', 'd', 'e', 'f', 'g', 'h', 'i']
>>> mylist2
['a', 'b', 'c', 'd', 'e', 'f', 'g', 'h', 'i']
>>> mylist2 [1:5]
['b', 'c', 'd', 'e']
>>>
```

You can always edit your entry, if you got the wrong files.

Let's say you want the 'f' values to be included in your print list, just make use of the code:

mylist2[1:6]

And press enter.

See image below:

```
Python 2.7.12 (v2.7.12:d33e0cf91556, Jun 27 2016, 15:19:22) [MSC v.1500 32 bit (
Intel)] on win32
Type "copyright", "credits" or "license()" for more information.
>>> mylist2=['a', 'b', 'c', 'd', 'e', 'f', 'g', 'h', 'i']
>>>
>>> mylist2
['a', 'b', 'c', 'd', 'e', 'f', 'g', 'h', 'i']
>>> mylist2 [1:6]
['b', 'c', 'd', 'e', 'f']
>>>
```

You can also use this statement, as a shortcut:

>   mylist2[1:]

Leaving the second value blank after the colon, will mean you want to access the values up to the last item in your particular list.

See the last portion of the image below:

```
Python 2.7.12 (v2.7.12:d33e0cf91556, Jun 27 2016, 15:19:22) [MSC v.1500 32 bit (Intel)] on win32
Type "copyright", "credits" or "license()" for more information.
>>> mylist2=['a', 'b', 'c', 'd', 'e', 'f', 'g', 'h', 'i']
>>>
>>> mylist2
['a', 'b', 'c', 'd', 'e', 'f', 'g', 'h', 'i']
>>> mylist2 [1:6]
['b', 'c', 'd', 'e', 'f']
>>>
>>> mylist2[1: ]
['b', 'c', 'd', 'e', 'f', 'g', 'h', 'i']
>>>
```

It could also be the other way around: You can leave the space before the colon blank to indicate that you want to access/print from 0 of the values.

Example:

>   mylist2[:7]

201

When you press 'enter' or execute, this will appear: See the last entry (bottom portion of the shell.

```
Python 2.7.12 Shell
File  Edit  Shell  Debug  Options  Window  Help
Python 2.7.12 (v2.7.12:d33e0cf91556, Jun 27 2016, 15:19:22) [MSC v.1500 32 bit (
Intel)] on win32
Type "copyright", "credits" or "license()" for more information.
>>> mylist2=['a', 'b', 'c', 'd', 'e', 'f', 'g', 'h', 'i']
>>>
>>> mylist2
['a', 'b', 'c', 'd', 'e', 'f', 'g', 'h', 'i']
>>> mylist2 [1:6]
['b', 'c', 'd', 'e', 'f']
>>>
>>> mylist2[1: ]
['b', 'c', 'd', 'e', 'f', 'g', 'h', 'i']
>>>
>>> mylist2[ :7]
['a', 'b', 'c', 'd', 'e', 'f', 'g']
>>>
```

You can print the whole list too, if you want, by leaving blanks, before and after the colon.

Example:

>mylist2 [:]

Press 'enter', and all the values in your list will be displayed. See image below:

You can also use the negative sequence of indexing, using the (-) sign. Please refer to the previous chapter.

Example:

If you want to slice your list to only 'h', you can enter in your shell this statement:

> mylist2 [-2:7]

You can also enter:

> mylist2 [-2:]

to print 'h' and 'i'.

See image below:

```
Python 2.7.12 Shell
File Edit Shell Debug Options Window Help
Python 2.7.12 (v2.7.12:d33e0cf91556, Jun 27 2016, 15:19:22) [MSC v.1500 32 bit (
Intel)] on win32
Type "copyright", "credits" or "license()" for more information.
>>>
>>> mylist2 = ['a', 'b', 'c', 'd', 'e', 'f', 'h', 'i']
>>> mylist2
['a', 'b', 'c', 'd', 'e', 'f', 'h', 'i']
>>>
>>> mylist2[ : ]
['a', 'b', 'c', 'd', 'e', 'f', 'h', 'i']
>>>
>>> mylist2[-2:7]
['h']
>>> mylist2[-2: ]
['h', 'i']
>>>
```

Skipping values in your list:

If you want to skip some values, you can use an additional colon to identify the values you want to skip.

Let's say you want to skip the values after every two intervals, you can use this code:

Example:

mylist2 [0:8:2]

Press 'enter', and the value, after every one interval, will be omitted from your results.

See image below:

```
>>>
>>>
>>> mylist2[0:8:2]
['a', 'c', 'e', 'h']
>>>
>>>
```

You can also make use of this code, if you want the same results (after every one interval).

>mylist2 [: :2]

When you press 'enter', you will be getting the same results. See image below:

```
>>>
>>>
>>>
>>> mylist2[ : :2]
['a', 'c', 'e', 'h']
>>>
>>>
```

You can use every 1, or 2 intervals, or any interval you want. Simply edit the code to obtain or print your desired results.

Example #2

If you have these assigned values to your list:

>mylist =[0, 1, 2, 3, 4, 5, 6, 7, 8, 9, 10, 11, 12, 13, 14, 15]

Press 'enter', and then type mylist to display your values. See image below:

```
                        Python 2.7.12 Shell
File  Edit  Shell  Debug  Options  Window  Help
Python 2.7.12 (v2.7.12:d33e0cf91556, Jun 27 2016, 15:19:22) [MSC v.1500 32 bit (
Intel)] on win32
Type "copyright", "credits" or "license()" for more information.
>>> mylist =[0, 1, 2, 3, 4, 5, 6, 7, 8, 9, 10, 11, 12, 13, 14, 15]
>>> mylist
[0, 1, 2, 3, 4, 5, 6, 7, 8, 9, 10, 11, 12, 13, 14, 15]
>>>
```

Take note that these numbers represent the indexes of your files. Hence, they may contain different data types, such as strings and other variables.

So, let's say you want to print/display files (indexes) 2 to 11 from your list, you can use a colon (:) to do this.

Example:

        mylist [2:12]

Press 'enter' or execute. The values from 2 to 11 will be displayed.

See image below:

```
Python 2.7.12 Shell
File Edit Shell Debug Options Window Help
Python 2.7.12 (v2.7.12:d33e0cf91556, Jun 27 2016, 15:19:22) [MSC v.1500 32 bit (
Intel)] on win32
Type "copyright", "credits" or "license()" for more information.
>>> mylist = [0, 1, 2, 3, 4, 5, 6, 7, 8, 9, 10, 11, 12, 13, 14, 15]
>>> mylist
[0, 1, 2, 3, 4, 5, 6, 7, 8, 9, 10, 11, 12, 13, 14, 15]
>>> mylist [2:12]
[2, 3, 4, 5, 6, 7, 8, 9, 10, 11]
>>>
```

In the example above, the list displayed is only up to 11, but you entered 12 in your statement. Hence, if you want your result to display up to 12, your statement should be:

mylist [2:13]

Press 'enter', or execute. The results will display your files from 2 to 12. Index 13 will not be displayed.

See image below:

```
Python 2.7.12 Shell
File  Edit  Shell  Debug  Options  Window  Help
Python 2.7.12 (v2.7.12:d33e0cf91556, Jun 27 2016, 15:19:22) [MSC v.1500 32 bit (
Intel)] on win32
Type "copyright", "credits" or "license()" for more information.
>>> mylist = [0, 1, 2, 3, 4, 5, 6, 7, 8, 9, 10, 11, 12, 13, 14, 15]
>>> mylist
[0, 1, 2, 3, 4, 5, 6, 7, 8, 9, 10, 11, 12, 13, 14, 15]
>>> mylist[2:12]
[2, 3, 4, 5, 6, 7, 8, 9, 10, 11]
>>>
>>> mylist[2:13]
[2, 3, 4, 5, 6, 7, 8, 9, 10, 11, 12]
>>>
```

These are the basic ways to slice your list. You will be able to learn more as you continue advancing in your knowledge of Python.

Explore

Now, try creating your own modules. Creating a python module can be easy or difficult depending on your ability to follow the advices given you.

Modules in python must have a .py extension to make it functional. Here are some tips you can use to create your module:

1. **Set up the framework of your module.**

    You can do this by getting hold of an already developed module and enhance it.

    Example:

```
cd modules/unsupported
cp example bird
```

2. Revise the files

You need to alter the files to fit the objective of your module.

3. Configure your pom.xml

Replace the word "example" with the title of your module :

```
<name>Example</name>
```

4. Add your code to the directory

5. Let others know that you are about to launch your module

This is important since this is a way of getting support from others who are into programming who can help you improve your module.

6. Run it/Test your module

Let your module run for the purpose you developed it. This is also to test whether your module is working or not

Did it work?

Hopefully, it did!

Chapter 29: Short Quiz on Python Programming

To test whether you have learned something from this book, here's a short quiz. Don't pressure yourself. Take a deep breath and relax. Learning should be fun. Take your time answering these questions without reviewing your notes.

You can write your answers on a piece of paper, or if you have already downloaded your free Python Programming application, you can answer the questions, using your interactive shell.

Questions:

1. You are tasked to prepare a Python program/module in welcoming college freshmen to your Business Administration Department. How can you let the students input their names, their ID numbers, and the time they came in, in the Python shell? How can you let them access your welcome message?"

2. What key can you use to convert an integer (number) to a string?

3. What is the simplest data/file form that is best in creating a list of names?

4. Create a Python statement that can print the following:

    a. A Tuple file named "taxRecord' that has these values: taxRecord=('first payment', 2015, 'second payment', 2016)

    names= ("John", "Bill", "Donna", "Ted", "Lance") + ages=(20, 30, 18, 25, 30)

b. items "c", "d", "e", "f" & "g" from this list: mylist=("a", "b", "c", "d", "e", "f", "g", "h", "I", "j")

   c. the length of this list: grocery = ('egg', 'sugar', 'milk', 'butter', 'flour')

5. How do you obtain the answer of 89^{12}, using a Python function key?

6. What is the Python function or key that you will use, if you want to remove a value from a list? Give one example.

7. Define concatenation. Give one example.

8. Create a Python statement based on the following:

   a. Print the contents of var1 30 times; var1=("Today is the day.")

   b. Access the built-in modules.

   c. Change the string file, 'records' to a Tuple file;

      records = ['Grace', 'Lancaster', 30, 'Metro St Chicago']

9. What is the difference between = and == ?

10. True or False: Python programming is an object-oriented language.

That's it!

Chapter 30: Answers to Short Quiz

Let's see if you got the correct answers. There may be slight differences for the various Python versions; nevertheless, it won't hurt you to learn about the answers.

ANSWERS:

1. This is one of the first lessons in the book – allowing a user to input some data.

   You can either click the Python shell directly from your saved Python file:

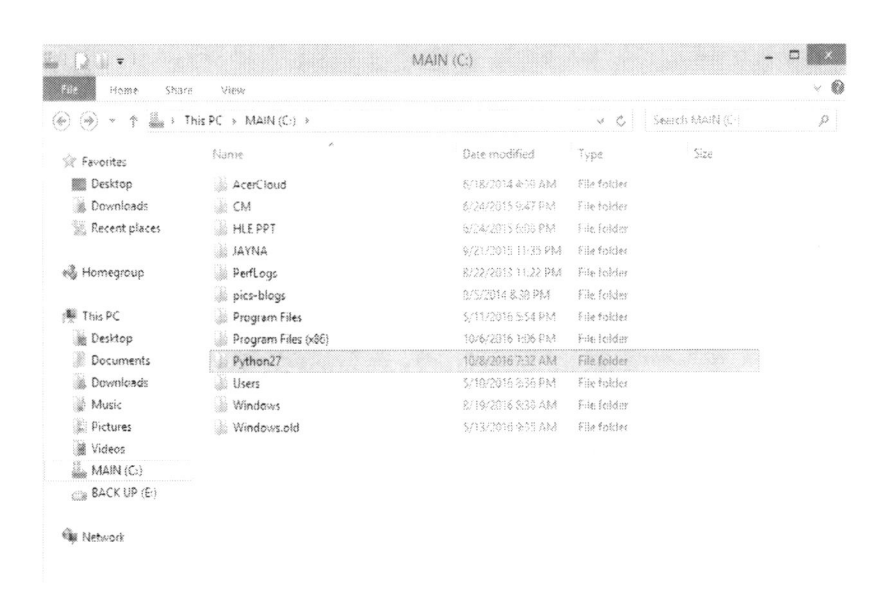

Then, click on python.

See image below:

To open your shell:

Or, you can do it the long way, but have a clearer and more maneuverable shell. Refer to chapter 7.

Let's say you have opened already your Python shell below using the long method:

```
Python 2.7.12 Shell
File  Edit  Shell  Debug  Options  Window  Help
Python 2.7.12 (v2.7.12:d33e0cf91556, Jun 27 2016, 15:19:22) [MSC v.1500 32 bit (
Intel)] on win32
Type "copyright", "credits" or "license()" for more information.
>>>
```

Open a 'New File' as instructed in chapter 7. Hence, you click 'File', and then 'New File' on the upper left hand corner of your shell. The new shell will appear:

```
Untitled
File  Edit  Format  Run  Options  Window  Help
```

In this new shell, you can edit all you want because pressing the 'enter' key won't return anything yet, unless you press or click the 'Run' menu. In this shell, you can now enter your Python statements.

The question is asking how you can allow the freshmen students to input their names, their ID numbers and the time they came in, and receive or access your welcome message.

The main fact to remember is that you use the 'input' key whenever you are asking the user to input or type something.

In your 'New File' shell, create these statements:

a=str(input("Please type your name and enclosed it in double quotes, an press enter."))

b=int(input("Please enter your ID number, and press enter."))

c=int(input("Please enter the time you came in, and press enter."))

print (max(a,b,c))

print ("Thank you. Welcome to the college of Business Administration, where learning is fun!")

Then you run this Python statement/code by clicking 'Run', and then 'Run Module'.

The first question will appear in a new shell. See image below:

Let's say the name of the student is Jean Walker, so she enters it. When she presses enter, the new question will appear:

217

Let's say the Jean's ID number is 3401. After she types in her ID, the next question will appear.

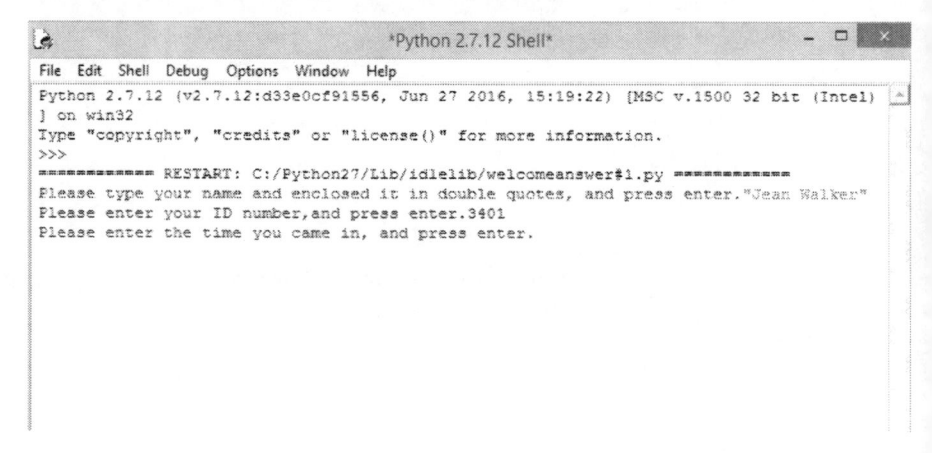

```
*Python 2.7.12 Shell*
File  Edit  Shell  Debug  Options  Window  Help
Python 2.7.12 (v2.7.12:d33e0cf91556, Jun 27 2016, 15:19:22) [MSC v.1500 32 bit (Intel)
] on win32
Type "copyright", "credits" or "license()" for more information.
>>>
============ RESTART: C:/Python27/Lib/idlelib/welcomeanswer#1.py ============
Please type your name and enclosed it in double quotes, and press enter."Jean Walker"
Please enter your ID number,and press enter.3401
Please enter the time you came in, and press enter.
```

If the time that she came in was 7, so she types it.

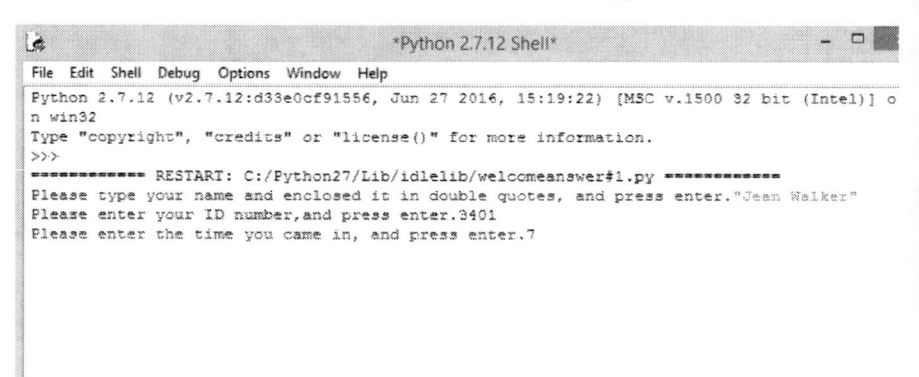

```
*Python 2.7.12 Shell*
File  Edit  Shell  Debug  Options  Window  Help
Python 2.7.12 (v2.7.12:d33e0cf91556, Jun 27 2016, 15:19:22) [MSC v.1500 32 bit (Intel)] o
n win32
Type "copyright", "credits" or "license()" for more information.
>>>
============ RESTART: C:/Python27/Lib/idlelib/welcomeanswer#1.py ============
Please type your name and enclosed it in double quotes, and press enter."Jean Walker"
Please enter your ID number,and press enter.3401
Please enter the time you came in, and press enter.7
```

After the student presses enter, this will appear:

```
                             Python 2.7.12 Shell                      _ □ ×
File  Edit  Shell  Debug  Options  Window  Help
Python 2.7.12 (v2.7.12:d33e0cf91556, Jun 27 2016, 15:19:22) [MSC v.1500 32 bit (Intel)] o
n win32
Type "copyright", "credits" or "license()" for more information.
>>>
============ RESTART: C:/Python27/Lib/idlelib/welcomeanswer#1.py ============
Please type your name and enclosed it in double quotes, and press enter."Jean Walker"
Please enter your ID number,and press enter.9401
Please enter the time you came in, and press enter.7
Jean Walker
Thank you. Welcome to the college of Business Administration, where learning is fun!
>>>
```

Of course, you will have to be there to assist. You have to save the file of each student after he is done, and 'Run Module' for the next student.

This would be tedious, but after this beginner's lesson, you may want to learn advance lessons later on, on how to embed the program and let it run by itself.

2. The key is str(int). For example you want to convert 10 to a string, you just use this statement: str(10).

3. The simplest best data/file form that is best in creating a list of names is a 'list'. This is because you can modify or update the information, if you want.

4. a. The Python statement in printing a Tuple file named "tacRecord" would be:

   taxRecord=('first payment', 2015, 'second payment', 2016)

   print "taxRecord"

219

```
>>>
>>>
>>> taxRecord=('first payment', 2015, 'second payment', 2016)
>>> print taxRecord
('first payment', 2015, 'second payment', 2016)
>>>
```

b. The Python statement/code would be:

    names= ("John", "Bill", "Donna", "Ted", "Lance")

    ages=(20, 30, 18, 25, 30)

    print (names + ages)

This will print/return your desired results:

```
Python 2.7.12 Shell
File Edit Shell Debug Options Window Help
Python 2.7.12 (v2.7.12:d33e0cf91556, Jun 27 2016, 15:19:22) [MSC v.1500 32 bit (
Intel)] on win32
Type "copyright", "credits" or "license()" for more information.
>>> names=("John", "Bill", "Donna", "Ted", "Lance")
>>> ages=(20, 30, 18, 25, 30)
>>> print (names+ages)
('John', 'Bill', 'Donna', 'Ted', 'Lance', 20, 30, 18, 25, 30)
>>>
>>>
```

c. The Python statement/code would be:

    mylist=("a", "b", "c", "d", "e", "f", "g", "h", "i", "j")
    print mylist[2:7]

    When you press 'enter', the items, "c", "d", "e", "f", & "g" will be printed from the list:

```
Python 2.7.12 Shell
File Edit Shell Debug Options Window Help
Python 2.7.12 (v2.7.12:d33e0cf91556, Jun 27 2016, 15:19:22) [MSC v.1500 32 bit (
Intel)] on win32
Type "copyright", "credits" or "license()" for more information.
>>> mylist=["a", "b", "c", "d", "e", "f", "g", "h", "i", "j"]
>>> print mylist[2:7]
('c', 'd', 'e', 'f', 'g')
>>>
>>>
```

d. The Python statement/command/code would be:

grocery = ("egg", "sugar", "milk", "butter", "flour")

print grocery

When you press 'enter', the results will be the printing of the items in your grocery list.

('egg', 'sugar', 'milk', 'butter', 'flour')

```
Python 2.7.12 Shell
File Edit Shell Debug Options Window Help
Python 2.7.12 (v2.7.12:d33e0cf91556, Jun 27 2016, 15:19:22) [MSC v.1500 32 bit (
Intel)] on win32
Type "copyright", "credits" or "license()" for more information.
>>> grocery = ("egg", "sugar", "milk", "butter", "flour")
>>> print grocery
('egg', 'sugar', 'milk', 'butter', 'flour')
>>>
>>>
```

Keep in mind that if you receive an error after pressing 'enter', your Python version may want you to use double quotes, so just edit your entries.

5. To obtain the answer of 89^{12} or 89 raised to the 12th power is to use the key 'pow'.

    Hence:

    pow=(89,12) or 89**12

    press 'enter' or 'Run', 'Run Module' (if 'New File').

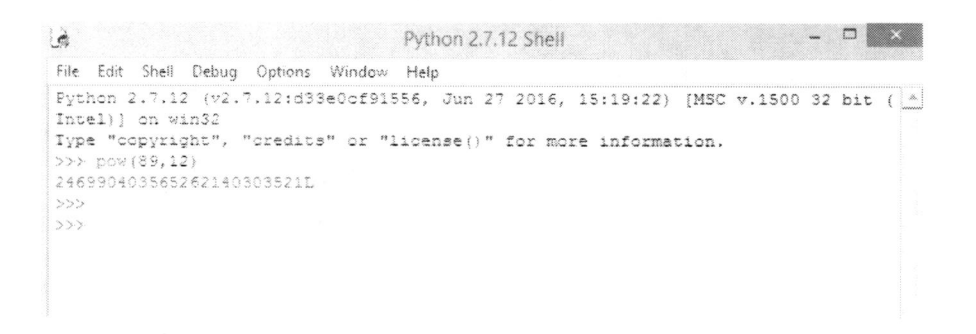

```
Python 2.7.12 (v2.7.12:d33e0cf91556, Jun 27 2016, 15:19:22) [MSC v.1500 32 bit (Intel)] on win32
Type "copyright", "credits" or "license()" for more information.
>>> pow(89,12)
246990403565262140303521L
>>>
>>>
```

6. The Python function or key to remove a value is 'remove'. Let's say your list is this: phone, diary, pen, notebook, pencil; and you want to remove diary from your list, here's how.

    Example:

    myList1=['phone', 'diary', 'pen', 'notebook', 'pencil']

```
                    Python 2.7.12 Shell
File Edit Shell Debug Options Window Help
Python 2.7.12 (v2.7.12:d33e0cf91556, Jun 27 2016, 15:19:22) [MSC v.1500 32 bit (
Intel)] on win32
Type "copyright", "credits" or "license()" for more information.
>>> myList1=['phone', 'diary', 'pen', 'notebook', 'pencil']
>>>
```

Now, remove 'diary' with this statement:

myList1.remove("diary")

```
                    Python 2.7.12 Shell
File Edit Shell Debug Options Window Help
Python 2.7.12 (v2.7.12:d33e0cf91556, Jun 27 2016, 15:19:22) [MSC v.1500 32 bit (
Intel)] on win32
Type "copyright", "credits" or "license()" for more information.
>>> myList1=['phone', 'diary', 'pen', 'notebook', 'pencil']
>>> myList1.remove('diary')
>>>
```

When you print it, the results will no longer show the value 'diary'. You can do this by entering the statement:

print myList1

And then press 'enter'. The results will print myLsit1 without 'diary'. See image below:

223

```
Python 2.7.12 Shell
File Edit Shell Debug Options Window Help
Python 2.7.12 (v2.7.12:d33e0cf91556, Jun 27 2016, 15:19:22) [MSC v.1500 32 bit (
Intel)] on win32
Type "copyright", "credits" or "license()" for more information.
>>> myList1=['phone', 'diary', 'pen', 'notebook', 'pencil']
>>> myList1.remove('diary')
>>> print myList1
['phone', 'pen', 'notebook', 'pencil']
>>>
>>>
```

7. In the Python language (as defined in chapter 3), **concatenation is** a series of connected strings or variables use in Python programs. The small strings can become larger strings through concatenation. This can be done using the 'join'( ) procedure, or the (+) sign. To replicate the string, you can use the asterisk (*) symbol, together with the number of how many times it should be replicated. (mystring1*10).

Example:

If you want the data: a, b, c and 4, 5, 6 to connect to each other, or to join each other. You can use the statement below:

['a', 'b', 'c'] + [4, 5, 6]

When you press 'enter', the two strings are already joined. See image below:

```
Python 2.7.12 Shell
File Edit Shell Debug Options Window Help
Python 2.7.12 (v2.7.12:d33e0cf91556, Jun 27 2016, 15:19:22) [MSC v.1500 32 bit (
Intel)] on win32
Type "copyright", "credits" or "license()" for more information.
>>> ['a', 'b', 'c'] + [4, 5, 6]
['a', 'b', 'c', 4, 5, 6]
>>>
>>> |
```

8. a. You can print the content of var1 30 times with the asterisk (*) function. The statement would be:

    var1=('Today is the day.')

    print var1*30

    ```
    >>>
    >>> var1=('Today is the day.')
    >>> var1*30
    >>> print var1*30
    Today is the day.Today is the day.Today is the day.Today is the day.Today is the day.Today is the day.Today is the day.Today is the day.Today is the day.Today i s the day.Today is the day.Today is the day.Today is the day.Today is the day.To day is the day.Today is the day.Today is the day.Today is the day.Today is the d ay.Today is the day.Today is the day.Today is the day.Today is the day.Today is the day.Today is the day.Today is the day.Today is the day.Today is the day.Toda y is the day.Today is the day.
    >>>
    >>>
    ```

    Hence, whether the value is an integer or a literal string, the (*) function works.

    If an error appears like this one: "SyntaxError: EOL (End of the Line) while scanning string literal", it means your strings are too long. You can do any of the following:

    - Check your quotes, change it to single or double quotes as the case maybe.
    - Check your distances between your values, they may be too far apart.
    - Check your quotes, some may have missing quotes or unmatched quotes.
    - Add the slash sign "\", if your values are too long, or the triple quotes if your statements are too long.

b. To access the built-in modules, the Python statement would be:

helpʼ('modules')

```
Python 2.7.12 Shell
File  Edit  Shell  Debug  Options  Window  Help
Python 2.7.12 (v2.7.12:d33e0cf91556, Jun 27 2016, 15:19:22) [MSC v.1500 32 bit (
Intel)] on win32
Type "copyright", "credits" or "license()" for more information.
>>> help('modules')
```

When you press enter, Python will ask you to wait as the program gathers all the built-in modules. You won't wait a minute because after several seconds, the results will return all the built-in modules. See image below:

```
Python 2.7.12 Shell
File  Edit  Shell  Debug  Options  Window  Help
Python 2.7.12 (v2.7.12:d33e0cf91556, Jun 27 2016, 15:19:22) [MSC v.1500 32 bit (
Intel)] on win32
Type "copyright", "credits" or "license()" for more information.
>>> help('modules')

Please wait a moment while I gather a list of all available modules...

1                   _locale             fileinput           pydoc
10                  _lsprof             findstring          pydoc_data
11                  _md5                fnmatch             pyexpat
12                  _msi                formatter           quopri
13                  _multibytecodec     fpformat            random
14                  _multiprocessing    fractions           re
16                  _osx_support        ftplib              repr
2                   _pyio               functools           rexec
4                   _random             future_builtins     rfc822
5                   _sha                gc                  rlcompleter
7                   _sha256             genericpath         robotparser
AutoComplete        _sha512             getopt              rpc
AutoCompleteWindow  _socket             getpass             run
AutoExpand          _sqlite3            gettext             runpy
BaseHTTPServer      _sre                glob                sched
Bastion             _ssl                grades2             select
Bindings            _strptime           gzip                sets
CGIHTTPServer       _struct             hashlib             setuptools
CallTipWindow       _subprocess         heapq               sgmllib
CallTips            _symtable           help                sha
Canvas              _testcapi           hmac                shelve
ClassBrowser        _threading_local    hotshot             shlex
CodeContext         _tkinter            htmlentitydefs      shutil
ColorDelegator      _warnings           htmllib             signal
```

c. You can change a string file to a Tuple file by simply using the function, tuple(str). The statement would be:

records = ['Grace','Lancaster',30,'Metro St Chicago']

tuple(records)

print tuple(records)

See image below:

```
records = ['Grace','Lancaster',30,'Metro St Chicago']
tuple(records)
print tuple(records)
```

This is a 'New File', so click 'Run", and then 'Run Module', and a new shell will open with the results. Your string file, 'records' is converted to a Tuple file.

227

```
                           Python 2.7.12 Shell                    _ □ X
File Edit Shell Debug Options Window Help
Python 2.7.12 (v2.7.12:d33e0cf91556, Jun 27 2016, 15:19:22) [MSC v.1500 32 bit (
Intel)] on win32
Type "copyright", "credits" or "license()" for more information.
>>>
================== RESTART: C:/Python27/Lib/idlelib/17.py ==================
('Grace', 'Lancaster', 30, 'Metro St Chicago')
>>>
```

9. The difference between = and == is that the = (equal sign) is used to give/assign values to data or files, while the == (double equal sign) is used to indicate that the values are equal.

10. True. Everything in Python refers to an object. That's its advantage over other programming language.

Now check your answers, and score yourself:

Here's how to score yourself:

1. 10 points

2. 3 points

3. 3 points

4. a. 5 points

   b. 5 points

   c. 5 points

5. 5 points

6. 5 points

7. 5 points

8. a. 3 points

   b. 3 points

   c. 4 points

9. 2 points

10. 2 points

Total points = 60

Score Interpretation:

60 points = Excellent! You're a genuine Python - follower.

You can now proceed to advance lessons.

45-59 points = Congratulations! You can be proud of your knowledge.

30-44 points = You've passed the test! You can do better though.

Keep going!

<30 points = Heads up! Failure is not permanent. It just means going

for it again, and again, until you succeed!

Chapter 31: Pointers in Using Python Programming

To optimize your use of the Python program as a beginner, here are significant pointers that can help your learning activity become fruitful.

1. **Be positive.** Anything new can be daunting – especially a 'foreign' language. Think about learning Korean, Chinese or Spanish, and you won't even want to start. But optimism can make you change your mind. As Master Yoda from "Star Wars' said: *"Do, there is no try."* Believe that you can do it, and you can. Think about all the benefits you can derive from what you will learn.

2. **Python is an extensive program; continue learning.** What we have discussed here is only the tip of the iceberg. There are still thousands of complex information about Python that you can learn.

3. **If you want to obtain several values from a list, use the 'slice' function**, instead of using the index. This is because the 'index' can provide you a single value only.

4. **Assign only integer values to indices.** Other number forms are not recognized by Python. Keep in mind that index values start from zero (0).

5. **Remember to use the 'help' function whenever necessary.** Explore the 'help' function, when in doubt on what to do. A little help from Python can go a long way.

6. **Python programming is a dynamic language.** Thus, you can experiment and come up with a code of your own to contribute towards its advancement.

7. **There are some differences among the Python versions**. But don't fret, the program itself has built-in modules and functions that can assist you in solving the problems you can encounter.

8. **The interactive shell can promptly return results**. That's why it's preferable to open a 'New File' first, before creating your statement. But if you're sure of your code, then, go ahead, and use the interactive shell directly.

9. **Separate your multiple statements, in a single line, with semicolons**. This is easier and more sensible.

10. **The three 'greater than' signs (>>>) or arrows is a prompt from the interactive shell.** You can explore their functionality as you create your statements.

11. **The Python interpreter can act as a calculator.** Using your interactive shell, you can compute math problems quickly – and continuously. No sweat!

12. **The # symbol indicates that the statement is a comment**. The # sign is placed before the comment, and after the Python statement, so Python won't mistake it as part of the statement or code.

13. **Use the reverse or back slash (\ ) to escape a single quote, or double quotes.** Examples of these are contracted words, such as 'don't, "won't", 'aren't'. When using them in Python, they will appear this way: 'don\'t', "won\'t", 'aren\'t'.

14. **A short cut in joining two literal strings (strings literal) is to put them beside each other and enclose each in quotes.** Example: 'Clinical' 'Chemistry'. This will give: ClinicalChemistry.

231

```
>>>
>>> 'Clinical' 'Chemistry'
'ClinicalChemistry'
>>>
>>>
>>>
```

15. **For modifying immutable data, create a new file.** These immutable data include strings, numbers, frozen set, bytes and Tuples. By creating a new file, you can modify, add and remove items from your immutable data.

Conclusion

The information in this book has the purpose of teaching you simple statements/codes that you can use easily.

It's expected that by this time, you can create the basic statements or codes for Python. In addition, you must be able to save and run your files on your own.

Remember to explore and test your short snippets of codes by using Python's interactive shell.

If you happen to be an expert, then the basic contents of this book may serve as reminders of the Python language.

For you, dear beginner, it's not a crime to go back to the chapters that you still could not comprehend.

By all means, you can read it twice, or as many times as you want.

After all, you can only truly learn about a new language, when you keep practicing.

Therefore, improve your knowledge by doing these three things regularly with Python: practice, practice and practice!

Bonus: Preview Of 'SQL The Ultimate Beginners Guide Learn SQL Today

For beginners, learning SQL is like learning how to speak a foreign language. You have to learn the alphabets first before you can successfully use it. Knowing the definition and purposes of SQL is crucial, before you, as a beginner can make any significant progress.

Looking at those symbols and queries may seem scary and confusing, but do not worry, the technical jargon is explained in the simplest manner to facilitate your comprehension.

What is SQL?

SQL stands for Structured Query Language. It is a standard programming language used in fetching or retrieving tables from databases. Other areas of use is creating, accessing and manipulating databases.

The most commonly used versions of the SQL are the SQL99 standard originally established by ANSI (American National Standards Institute). There is also an ORACLE version called PL/SQL, and a Microsoft version called T-SQL or Transact-SQL.

More people are growing aware of it because SQL is one of the easiest and most powerful methods of editing databases. It works in such a way that you can perform your tasks more efficiently, within a shorter timeframe.

The SQL's basis is the RDBMS (Relational Database Management System), which stores data in the form of tables.